"Randy Kulman has developed a practical, accessible resource for teens that honors their positive experiences with screen time while simultaneously engaging them, through interactive exercises, in meaningful reflections about the costs and benefits of excessive use. Informed by current research, this book is just what parents and other adults need to address concerns about technology use in a positive, respectful way."

—**Jon Lasser, PhD**, professor of school psychology at Texas State University, and coauthor of *Tech Generation*

"Gaming is a complex world with confusing narratives about games' supposed ills and considerable benefits. With his new, excellent workbook for youth, *The Gaming Overload Workbook*, Randy Kulman gives youth a fun and insightful opportunity to look at games through a whole new lens! Highly recommended for kids who love games."

—**Chris Ferguson, PhD**, professor of psychology at Stetson University, and longtime researcher on the effects of videogames

"Randy Kulman's workbook is a critically important resource for adolescents, parents, and clinicians concerned about the impact that gaming may have on teens' lives. Using a unique blend of science, clinical experience, and recommendations from teenagers, this workbook is an indispensable guide to balancing video game playing, screen use, and important life activities. Teens and their families can use this workbook to develop a healthy and balanced 'play diet.'"

—**George J. DuPaul, PhD**, professor of school psychology, and associate dean for research at Lehigh University; and author of books and scientific journal articles regarding attention deficit/hyperactivity disorder (ADHD)

"Randy Kulman has created an innovative workbook for teens to better understand digital gaming. His unique approach will engage teens on their level to better understand the skills they are learning through gaming, but also to understand the risks of overload. With real case presentations, they will learn how to balance digital play. I am excited to share this book with my patients who struggle with gaming overload."

—**Celeste Corcoran, MD, FAAP**, primary care pediatrician with thirty-two years' experience, faculty at the Warren Alpert Medical School of Brown University, and diplomate in obesity medicine

"*The Gaming Overload Workbook* will be a treasured resource for teens, their parents, and their teachers. Randy Kulman provides a unique way to help evaluate the impact of screen time and video games on teen behavior, problem-solving, time management, learning, and socialization. Numerous activities contained in the workbook invite teens to engage in self-analysis of their screen-time behavior, and encourage them to draw conclusions about how their video play impacts them. Kulman has written extensively on this topic, and his new workbook gives teens an opportunity to identify the positive and negative impacts that video games and screen time can have. I highly recommend this exceptional and highly practical book."

—**Harvey C. Parker, PhD**, clinical psychologist in South Florida; cofounder of Children and Adults with Attention-Deficit/Hyperactivity Disorder (CHADD); author of several books and publications on child development; and recipient of a CHADD Lifetime Achievement Award

the gaming overload workbook

a teen's guide to balancing screen time, video games & real life

RANDY KULMAN, PhD

Instant Help Books
An Imprint of New Harbinger Publications, Inc.

Publisher's Note

This publication is designed to provide accurate and authoritative information in regard to the subject matter covered. It is sold with the understanding that the publisher is not engaged in rendering psychological, financial, legal, or other professional services. If expert assistance or counseling is needed, the services of a competent professional should be sought.

Distributed in Canada by Raincoast Books

Copyright © 2020 by Randy Kulman
          Instant Help Books
          An imprint of New Harbinger Publications, Inc.
          5674 Shattuck Avenue
          Oakland, CA 94609
          www.newharbinger.com

Cover design by Amy Shoup

Acquired by Jess O'Brien

Edited by Karen Schader

Library of Congress Cataloging-in-Publication Data

Names: Kulman, Randy, 1955- author.
Title: The gaming overload workbook : a teen's guide to balancing screen time, video games, and real life / Randy Kulman.
Description: Oakland, CA : New Harbinger Publications, [2020] | Series: Instant help books | Includes bibliographical references. | Audience: Ages 14-18.
Identifiers: LCCN 2020004632 (print) | LCCN 2020004633 (ebook) | ISBN 9781684035519 (paperback) | ISBN 9781684035526 (pdf) | ISBN 9781684035533 (epub)
Subjects: LCSH: Video games and teenagers--Juvenile literature. | Video games--Psychological aspects--Juvenile literature. | Video game addiction--Prevention--Juvenile literature.
Classification: LCC HQ784.V53 K849 2020 (print) | LCC HQ784.V53 (ebook) | DDC 794.80835--dc23
LC record available at https://lccn.loc.gov/2020004632
LC ebook record available at https://lccn.loc.gov/2020004633

Printed in the United States of America

22   21   20

10   9   8   7   6   5   4   3   2   1   First Printing

Contents

a letter to teens

If you're reading this book, you probably like playing video games. It could be that you're reading it so you can tell your friends about the benefits of playing video games. Or maybe your parents gave you the book because they think you're too focused on playing video games. Perhaps you even think you shouldn't spend so much time playing video games.

It's common for teenagers to be told that they spend too much of their time and energy playing video games or staring at their cell phones. And it's not just parents and teachers telling them to put down their screens. More than half of teenagers express concerns about how much time they spend playing video games. Many of you may feel that you should be doing something else but have difficulty putting away your screens. While most teens see their time playing video games and using technology as beneficial, more than half report that not everything about screen time is positive. And unfortunately, some teens may find themselves addicted to video games.

As a psychologist, my passion has always been to learn about children's and teenagers' play. I can tell you that play in any form is an incredibly important thing for you because it's one of the best ways to learn. And that includes a twenty-first-century type of play: video games.

The biggest problem with video games is *not* that you can't learn all kinds of skills and knowledge, socialize with others, or have fun and challenge your brain—but that video games and other technologies can be hard to ignore and sometimes don't leave enough time for other important things.

You can do something about this, but it's a tough battle! One of the main reasons it's so difficult to limit play is that game developers have designed video games to keep you on screens as long as possible. Game publishers and designers use many psychological strategies in this process, because the more you play, the more money they make. Sometimes it's hard to figure out how to quit playing, even when you would like to stop. Reading this book will help you determine if you're playing too much. One of the great things about this book is that I was able to interview many teenagers about how they manage video-game overload, and most of the suggestions you'll see about dealing with overload come from them.

Another important part of this book describes the positive things you can get from playing video games. It's not reasonable to think that video games are going to disappear any time soon, so it's really important for you to learn how to make the most of your video-game play. This book will show you how video-game play can make you more creative, help you learn about your world, and assist you in developing deeper relationships with your friends. You'll also discover how video games can teach you problem-solving skills, help you become more flexible, and improve skills such as planning and organization.

However, if your only play involves video games, you won't have time for other play activities that are really important for personal growth and development. In this book, I'll guide you to having a healthy and balanced "play diet" in which physical, social, creative, and free play are regular parts of your life. I'll also show you how you can use your interest in video games and other screen-based play to expand your interests. Instead of avoiding your technology, you'll discover how to use it as a tool to improve yourself.

My goal is that young people who read this book will think more about the role that video games play in their lives. I also hope that this book prompts readers to talk to their peers, parents, and teachers about how video-game play impacts their present and future. After reading this book, you might find that you have a lot to teach your parents and other adults about this topic.

a letter to clinicians, educators, and parents

The Gaming Overload Workbook is a vehicle to prompt discussion with teenagers about the use of video games and other screen-based technologies. It's not intended as a book that tells teenagers to avoid the "horrors" of playing video games. Instead, it's written to help teenagers and adults have an open discussion about the role video games play in their lives.

It might appear to adults that teenagers spend all their time glued to screens and that, if given the choice, adolescents might devote their entire day to playing video games and checking their social media feeds. However, when asked about their screen time, many teenagers have misgivings. A fascinating study conducted by the Pew Research Center in 2018 indicates that more than half of teenagers report concerns about the amount of time they spend with video games and other technologies. These teens don't need their parents to tell them that they're overly involved with their screens, but they may not have the resources or strategies to change this. This study and others suggest that while some teens may want to cut back on video-game play, they find it extremely difficult to do.

The Gaming Overload Workbook does not blame teenagers for this problem. The reality is that game publishers, technology companies, and social media giants have expertly designed their technologies to keep both kids (and adults) engaged with screens as often and for as long as possible. The basic business model for almost all these technologies is to keep as many eyes on their product for as long as they can. Sometimes they don't know how to make money from you at first, but they all seem to figure it out.

It's not just with video games that overload occurs. Social media, streaming TV and gaming services, podcasts, and online shopping are all designed to keep you engaged. And beyond the "software" is the hardware—the smartphones that never shut off and are designed so you can't leave home (or anywhere else) without them. This is likely to get worse as virtual assistants become ubiquitous. Technology companies have made their tools inescapable and, to some degree, irresistible, as described by marketing expert Adam Alter in his book by the same name (2017). It's tough enough for adults to manage this overwhelming influence; imagine what it's like for teens and younger children.

This workbook is written for teenagers who love playing video games, some of whom may occasionally spend too much time in their game play. Another target of this book is teens who identify themselves as gamers, whose social relationships are often based on their connections with other game players, and whose major form of entertainment is playing video games. These teens might be best described as passionate or engaged gamers. For the vast majority of gamers, video games are a net asset to their lives, adding enjoyment, social opportunities, and cognitive challenges. But due to the draw of games and technology, even some of these teens may be sacrificing fundamental activities such as exercise, creative play, and time in nature that are essential to a healthy lifestyle.

More alarming are gamers who are better described as obsessive, problematic, or addicted, for whom gaming has become a serious health problem. While these teens constitute a small minority, their video-game play is causing them to markedly sacrifice other activities and interfering with basic functions such as getting enough sleep, completing homework, or spending face-to-face time with others. These teens need help from parents, clinicians, and educators in rebalancing their activities.

Part of the philosophy of *The Gaming Overload Workbook* is to encourage teens who love playing video games to consider how they might take their passion and convert it into future educational opportunities and jobs. Some of these gamers may aspire to become video-game testers or developers, while others may dream of becoming professional gamers. With players and esports teams earning millions of dollars for winning tournaments, this dream is understandable, although the current chances of becoming a professional gamer are significantly less than those of becoming a professional football player. However, there are many other ways to use game-based skills in the broad fields of technology and computer sciences, and many high-paying and stimulating jobs are available now and will be in the near future.

This workbook takes the perspective that games and technology are not inherently good or bad, and instead presents a realistic view of twenty-first-century life, recognizing that these technologies are here to stay. In my previous work, I've written extensively about the importance of play in children's learning. *The Gaming Overload Workbook* views digital play, the use of video games and other technologies, as one of the five major forms of play seen in twenty-first-century kids. Social, physical, creative, and unstructured play are the other major types of play. Unfortunately, because of its allure, digital play has broadly displaced other types of play. Rather than focusing on the evils of video games and technology, my approach, which is seen in many of the activities, is to help teens and parents work toward creating a healthy and balanced "play diet" in which teens exercise, get outdoors, spend face-to-face time with others, and dedicate time to being creative and mindful.

I am hopeful that this book will help bring families closer together and assist teens with integrating healthy video-game play into their lives. Games and technologies are not going away, but neither is the need for exercise, face-to-face communication, and spending time in nature. Helping teens explore these concerns and have healthy conversations with those they trust is the goal of this book. Many of the suggestions for activities came from my clinical work with patients, interviews with college students who love gaming, and professionals in the larger gaming community. I welcome your observations and thoughts about how we can help our children and teenagers avoid overload while they continue to engage in healthy, constructive video-game play; you can use the contact form at learningworksforkids.com to share them.

1 playing video games

Spence has always liked playing video games. His favorite game when he was younger was Mario Kart, and when he got a little older, he began playing Harry Potter and Star Wars games with his younger brother. His parents, who thought he should be studying all the time, would ask him to stop playing, but he wouldn't listen to them because he was so involved with the game. As he got older, he began to play more first-person shooters, and playing online games such as League of Legends, Overwatch, and Fortnite is one of the ways he connects with his friends after school. Playing video games has not impacted his grades; he is even on pace to become his school valedictorian. He doesn't think his parents understand how much he has learned from playing video games or how important they are in building his friendships.

for you to know

Did you know that in 2018, according to a study reported by the Pew Research Center, 97 percent of teenage boys and 83 percent of teenage girls in the United States played video games? About 33 percent of the boys identified themselves as gamers, compared to only 9 percent of the girls. Video gaming is obviously a very popular activity. Many studies have demonstrated that playing about an hour a day can be good for the brain, improve one's learning capacity, and develop critical-thinking skills. Of course, it matters what types of games people play, how much they play, and if their game play gets in the way of accomplishing other things in their lives. Let's learn a bit about what you're doing with your video-game play.

for you to do

Put a check in the column that shows how often you play each type of game.

	Never	Sometimes	Often
Puzzle			
Strategy			
Action/adventure			
First-person shooters			
Role-playing			
Sports or racing games			
Educational			
Simulation games			

Write down four games that have been your favorites in the past year, and check whether they are single or multiplayer games.

Jot down your ideas as to whether games are isolating you from others or connecting you with your friends. Consider how many games you play with school or community friends as opposed to online friends.

_____

_____

_____

more to do

One of the most important concerns about video games and other screen activities is the amount of time kids, teens, and adults spend with their screens. While we explore these issues in later chapters, let's get an initial estimate of the amount of time you spend with different types of screen-based activities. Do you play more or less on school days as opposed to nonschool days?

Estimate how many minutes you spend on each of the following activities:

	On school days	On days off from school
Homework on computer or screen		
Playing video games		
Watching network or cable TV		
Streaming (Netflix, Hulu, Disney+)		
Listening to music		
Social media (Instagram, Snapchat)		
Texting		
Talking on my cell phone		
Video chats		
Surfing the internet		
Listening to music		

are you addicted to video games? 2

Bruce wonders if he is addicted to video games. He's the kind of kid who really gets into what he's doing. For example, he's a voracious reader. When he was nine, he didn't just read the Harry Potter series, he read it five times and was able to remember scads of details from all seven books. When he began playing basketball, he really got into it and played intensely, even though he wasn't that good.

In the past year, he has gotten into a few online games. He likes esports and is becoming an accomplished team player for League of Legends *and* Overwatch. *Because he lives on the East Coast, he often finds himself playing with his West Coast teammates late into the night. He looks forward to weekends, when he can play most of the day and much of the night.*

Bruce has been able to keep his grades up because school has always been easy for him. At first, his parents didn't notice how much he was playing video games because his homework was getting done, and the 100s on tests kept rolling in. But lately they've become worried because he has always had an addictive quality to his interests, and his fascination with gaming appears to be more intense than previous obsessions. Bruce has noticed this himself. He finds himself thinking about his game play while at school, and it has begun to interfere with his social activities on weekends.

His parents are also concerned that he has begun to gain weight due to sitting around playing video games. They want to take him to a psychiatrist who specializes in youngsters with addiction to video games, but Bruce thinks psychiatrists are weird and refuses to go.

for you to know

For the past few decades, parents and doctors have been concerned that kids and adults can become addicted to playing video games. You might also be concerned for yourself or a friend. People who are truly addicted to video games find that their game play causes problems in many parts of their life. They want to play video games all day long; think about them constantly; and lie, take risks, and give up other interests to play.

Although not all doctors agree, there is now an official diagnosis for people who become addicted to video games: internet gaming disorder. It's important to recognize that this disorder is quite rare, and many psychologists and clinicians question whether it is a quantifiable diagnosis. Even those doctors who use the diagnosis agree that it's very rare among teenagers. According to a 2017 article in *Pediatrics*, most teenagers who play too many video games don't warrant a diagnosis of this disorder, as it occurs in only approximately 5 percent of the population. But don't forget—some teens may not be "addicted" to video games, but still find that their game play is causing problems in specific areas of their life.

for you to do

Most teens who play video games aren't addicted to gaming. Even teens who game too much may not be technically addicted, and video-game addiction is something that only a psychiatrist can officially diagnose. In this workbook, we invite you to look more closely at your gaming habits, but we also want to be extremely careful not to use this knowledge to make an inappropriate self-diagnosis. When someone learns something about a new condition or disease, it's really common to self-diagnose based on a small amount of knowledge. In fact, this tendency is so common that it has a name: medical student disease. This is because many medical students learn something in class, notice a minor characteristic of a disorder in themselves, and then exaggerate its significance.

Please do not make this same mistake. The questions below are meant to help you better understand how gaming affects the rest of your life so that you can get the most out of the activities in this workbook.

On a scale of 0 to 3 (0 = never, 1 = sometimes, 2 = often, 3 = daily, rate how often you find yourself doing each of the following:

_____ Thinking about game play while in school or with your friends

_____ Identifying with video gaming more than other parts of your life

_____ Getting very upset when you can't play video games

_____ Feeling like you never have enough time to play games

_____ Being less interested in sports, friends, and your previous hobbies

_____ Getting stressed because game play has created problems in other areas of your life

_____ Being dishonest with yourself, friends, or family about how much you are playing

_____ Getting in trouble because you spend too much money on gaming

_____ Relying upon gaming as your go-to activity for getting away from it all

_____ Taking risks to continue gaming, such as putting off studying until you are too tired to study

_____ Not completing schoolwork and other obligations due to gaming

_____ Taking less care of your physical health (not getting enough sleep, eating junk food, forgetting to shower) because of gaming

Now, add up your score. Scores can range from a low of 0 to a high of 36. Caution! This rating is only a guide to help in understanding the negative impact of excessive gaming. If your score is above 26, please use the exercises in this workbook, and talk to your parents, teachers, or doctors about your gaming. Most of the activities in this workbook are for teens who sometimes overload on gaming, so if your score is 25 or under, you can still learn a lot about healthy gaming habits from the rest of this workbook.

more to do

Many teens who love video games can play too much but don't have internet gaming disorder. Gaming may sometimes interfere with homework completion or sleep but is not causing any damage to their family, social, and academic lives. Some of these individuals are proud to identify themselves as *gamers*. Psychologists have come up with a few other labels for teens and adults who love video games. Your score from the above scale can be used as a rough estimate to see if any of these terms fit your gaming identity.

Problem gamers (scores of 19–25): These individuals spend much (and, according to others, too much) of their time playing video games, and gaming causes some conflicts and problems in their lives. They don't show the symptoms of gamers who are more addicted, such as anxiety and withdrawal. If this fits you, tell how.

_____

_____

_____

_____

Passionate or obsessed gamers (scores of 13–18): These individuals love gaming, are devoted to the craft of gaming, and spend much of their time thinking about their game play. If this fits you, tell how.

_____

_____

_____

_____

Engaged gamers (scores of 8–12): These individuals love gaming and want to develop expertise as gamers, but do not show any negative side effects of it. They continue to perform well across all other areas of their lives. If this fits you, tell how.

_____

_____

_____

_____

3 why you play video games

Leslie is always the first of her friends to try out new games and technology. She's a whiz at computer programming and using social media. But mostly, she describes herself as a gamer. She enjoys playing games because they're fun, challenging, and always changing.

Minecraft was her favorite game when she was younger because there were very few rules and she could choose to do whatever she wanted to in the game. She thinks playing Minecraft makes her more creative and a better problem solver. She believes that her current interest in travel and world history is a direct result of playing so many hours of Minecraft. She's also told her parents that Minecraft helped make her interested in building and construction. Her parents hope that it might lead to an interest in their family real estate business.

for you to know

There are some very good reasons why kids love video games. Beyond their entertainment value, the games most teenagers like best are not the ones that are easy to beat but the more complex ones in which challenges, adversity, and failure are common. Video games are great tools for learning because they are "hard" fun. Games and activities that are both playful and difficult often provide the best opportunities for learning and becoming motivated to improve yourself. This describes many of the best video games.

Surveys of teenagers have found many other reasons they love video games, including the challenge of figuring things out, relief from stress, and an outlet for anger. In her book *Reality Is Broken*, game designer Jane McGonigal describes how games make us happy because they are "hard work that we choose for ourselves" (2011). Gamers tend to stick to very difficult games as long as they feel capable of meeting the challenge.

One of the reasons many psychologists view video gaming positively is that they recognize that play is crucial for learning. Play (including video gaming) is important for children and teenagers to learn about their world, solve problems, and develop critical social skills.

for you to do

Rate the importance of these reasons for playing video games:

	Not important	Somewhat important	Very important
Learning about the world			
Relieving stress			
Releasing my anger			
Having fun			
The challenge of winning			
Competing with others			
Hanging out with my friends			
Making me feel better about myself			
Relieving boredom			

You might find that video games are not just fun but also add to the quality of your life. Some teenagers report that they play games instead of engaging in other activities because gaming improves their social and emotional lives. If this is the case for you, describe some of the ways that video-game playing enriches your life.

_____

_____

_____

_____

_____

more to do

Complete this exercise using two of your favorite video games.

Game 1: _____

Why I like playing it: _____

_____

Its benefits and drawbacks for:

• Teaching me about the world

_____

_____

- Relieving my stress

  _____

  _____

- Releasing anger

  _____

  _____

- Helping me have fun

  _____

  _____

- Teaching me to compete

  _____

  _____

- Getting me to hang out with friends

  _____

  _____

- Improving my self-esteem

  _____

  _____

- Relieving boredom

  _____

  _____

Game 2: _____

Why I like playing it: _____

_____

Its benefits and drawbacks for:

- Teaching me about the world

  _____

  _____

- Relieving my stress

  _____

  _____

- Releasing anger

  _____

  _____

- Helping me have fun

  _____

  _____

- Teaching me to compete

  _____

  _____

- Getting me to hang out with friends

  _____

  _____

- Improving my self-esteem

  _____

  _____

- Relieving boredom

  _____

  _____

4　when play gets in the way

Billy loves playing first-person shooters (FPS) and has been playing them since he was ten. He's always been a fan of the Call of Duty games and then got into playing Fortnite. Undoubtedly, he'll play the next super popular online FPS that comes out. Billy enjoys the competition and camaraderie that go with playing these games, and while he has other interests (for example, playing guitar and being the second baseman on his championship baseball team), he gets most excited when he has a chance to hang out on his computer and play games nonstop.

Unfortunately, he sometimes plays late into the night, leaving little time for homework and definitely not enough time for sleep. He likes to go to bed after midnight and wake up later in the morning, but school gets in the way. Lately he's been increasingly tired at school and in his other activities. He's always been an A student but has gotten behind in one of his classes and might need to take an incomplete and finish it during the summer. He realizes that staying up too late playing video games is causing some difficulties for him and that he really ought to do something about it.

for you to know

A majority of teenagers are aware that they sometimes spend too much time playing video games or being on their screens. While you might not be talking about this with your friends, the Pew Research Center (2018) reports that more than 50 percent of teens have taken steps to cut back on their phone use, and 58 percent have tried to reduce the amount of time they play video games. You might have heard your parents express concerns about how much time you spend playing video games and checking your phone. Insightful teenagers don't need their parents to harass them about screen time; they're already aware of how much time they spend with this. As you'll learn from reading this book, part of the reason that teenagers (and their parents!) find it so difficult to put away their devices is the brilliance of programmers, game publishers, and other technology companies in keeping you enchanted with your screens. The more time you spend on your screen, the more opportunity there is to sell you something or for technology companies to learn what you like to do.

Recent studies of teenagers' use of video games and screen time have shown that teenagers have become more astute observers of their screen time and that of their peers and parents. In the same Pew study, 51 percent of teenagers reported that they often or sometimes found their parents to be distracted by their own cell phones when they were trying to have conversations with them. Have your parents ever criticized you for the same transgression? Get ready for us to explore this topic in detail in activity 6.

for you to do

Complete this chart to show how often video-game play or screen time interferes with the following activities:

	Never	Once a week	Two to three times a week	Daily
Getting enough sleep				
Completing my homework				
Being on time for activities				
Being fully engaged in conversation with others				
Finishing my chores at home				
Staying focused in the classroom				
Having time to hang out with friends in real life				

more to do

Select one of the above areas (for example, sleep, homework, or focus) where video-game play and screen time get in your way at least two to three times per week. Choose an area that reflects your own concerns rather than ones identified by your parents or teachers. Once you've chosen, focus on the aspects that you can control. For example, you probably can't control how much homework you get, but you do have some choice about when and where to do it.

What can you do when video games and screens get in your way? Come up with ideas that go beyond reducing your time spent with screens, and think about small steps that would help you achieve your goals.

_____

_____

_____

_____

_____

5 bingeing on your screen

Joy is seventeen and a big fan of classic video games and TV programs, especially early Mario and Sonic games. As a child, she watched reruns of her favorite programs on TV and was a huge fan of sitcoms. She loves using her classic NES and Sega consoles.

She was overjoyed when her parents purchased Netflix for their home. Instead of watching shows one at a time when they were scheduled on Nick at Nite, she could watch many seasons of her favorite old shows nonstop. She had always remembered the characters very well, and now she could use her excellent memory to reenact some of the dialogue from the shows.

Joy has also recently begun to watch some of the new TV series produced by Netflix. She enjoys sharing her favorites with her many friends and has become their go-to source for the best new series as well as for knowing the best games for the classic NES console. Occasionally she overdoes it and binge-watches, but her parents don't seem to care because they've also become binge-watchers of their favorite shows.

for you to know

Before there were concerns about kids spending too much time playing video games, parents were worried about the impact of TV viewing on their children's brains. Concerns about kids watching TV have been around since the 1950s and '60s, when most families had small black-and-white TV sets, and there were only three major networks. TV was described as a "vast wasteland" where the majority of programming consisted of cookie-cutter cop shows, situation comedies, and westerns. Children's programming was primarily available on Saturday mornings. When children couldn't find a show they wanted to watch on one of the three channels, they found something else to do. In the 1960s, there was a panic about TV viewing harming children's eyesight. Even with only three stations to watch, parents and educators were concerned that kids were spending too much time with TV.

Today, thousands of TV channels are available, and while some families still obtain their TV service through rooftop antennas (do you know what those are?), TV access is often through cable companies, streaming services, or directly on the internet. Watching what you want when you want it has become the norm. Livestreaming, YouTube videos, Hulu, Disney+, Netflix, and Twitch.tv have become staples and substitutes for previous forms of TV viewing.

Perhaps even more remarkable to your parents or grandparents is how you access TV and videos. The ability to watch virtually any TV programming on your mobile devices or on a variety of other screens means that your parents probably no longer know what you're viewing, which can make them scared. Keep that in mind when they want to know what you're watching on your screens.

for you to do

Think about the role that TV plays in the life of your family.

What type of TV shows bring your family together?

_____

_____

Do you use the TVs in your home to play video games? Watch YouTube? Go online?

_____

_____

If you ever binge-watch, write about why. If you don't, ask friends or family members who binge-watch and learn more about why they do so.

_____

_____

_____

To what degree is watching TV a go-to relaxation activity for you? For your family? How does it impact your family relationships?

_____

_____

_____

more to do

Consider some of the ways that TV can be a positive influence for you in your day-to-day activities. If you don't use it in any of these ways, think about how you might leverage your TV watching to improve yourself.

Complete this chart to show how often watching TV has helped you in these ways:

	Never	Rarely	Sometimes	Often
Getting exercise (for example, riding an exercise bike or using an elliptical at home or in the gym)				
Being more social by getting together with friends for a TV event				
Inspiring a new interest (for example, wanting to learn more about world history or science)				
Being part of a family activity that joins me with my parents or siblings				
Being more creative (for example, in my writing for school, my involvement in a drama club, or learning more about comedy				
Maintaining an interest in current events (for example, by watching news programs, political debates, or shows about public health issues or the environment)				
Engaging in activities and interests outside of school (for example, following a sports team on TV, watching a hiking or survival series, or seeing a movie that prompted me to read the book it was based on)				

activity 5 ✳ bingeing on your screen

Now that you have examined these possibilities, create a list of specific ways that TV has been a positive force in your life.

_____

_____

_____

_____

Lauren loves her cell phone—when it's not broken and when she can find it. She's always been attached to her phone because it helps her communicate with others and keep connected with her friends from all over the world. But as she's gotten older, she uses her phone less to text, talk, and check social media. More often, she uses it to keep up with current events, play a few simple video games, and pursue other interests such as music and social-justice issues.

As Lauren has changed her screen habits, she's started to notice other people's use of screens and technology. She sees that her mother's phone is always by her side and that when she isn't playing Candy Crush Saga or Words with Friends, she's constantly checking her Facebook feed. Her mother also spends hours talking on the phone to Lauren's aunts and uncles. Lauren notices that her stepfather can watch football nonstop for eight hours every Sunday of the NFL season. And occasionally, she and her mother do some binge-watching of popular Netflix shows.

Lauren is a bit cynical about adults who express concerns about how teenagers waste their time playing video games or staring at their cell phones. She sees some hypocrisy in how many parents (although, interestingly, not hers) complain about excessive screen time in teenagers. As far as she's concerned, her parents and the parents of many of her peers are too busy playing video games and focusing on screens rather than on other people.

for you to know

Did you know that, on average, adults spend nine hours and twenty-two minutes a day with screen-based media? More than three hours of that is spent watching TV, DVDs, and videos, while about one and a half hours is spent playing video games.

Your parents might like to tell you that most of their daily screen time is work related, but a 2016 study conducted by Common Sense Media, which explores screen and media consumption in children, found that only one hour and thirty-nine minutes of adult screen time is spent on work-related tasks each day.

What's most fascinating about these statistics is the similarity between the use of screen time in adults and teens. A 2015 Common Sense Media study found that teens—who report an average of eight hours and fifty-six minutes a day of screen time—spend less time with their screens than adults do. Even stranger is that many parents who want their kids to spend less time with screens think that they are providing a good example for their kids. Seventy-eight percent of parents believe that they are good media and technology role models for their children. Forty-three percent of parents believe their kids spend too much time online, and 38 percent think their kids overshare personal details. What do you think?

for you to do

Without announcing what you are doing, monitor your parents' screen time for one week. You can use the chart below (or download a copy at http://www.newharbinger.com/45519), or keep track on your phone, using an app such as Harvest, Toggl, or Tracking Time. Obviously, you won't be with your parents 24/7, so keep track of only what you see. Initially, choose the parent who appears to use technology most often. (You can track your other parent the following week if you choose.) Don't hover over on them; just record what you observe. Add some detail that goes beyond just the amount of time they spent in front of screens; for example, note if they are using their phones during meals or constantly checking their social media.

activity 6 ✳ what your parents do with video games and screen time

My Parents' Screen Time

Day	Amount of time	Description
Monday		
Tuesday		
Wednesday		
Thursday		
Friday		
Saturday		
Sunday		

more to do

At the same time you're monitoring your parents' screen time, ask them to do the same thing for themselves. If you use a time-tracking app in your analysis, you might even suggest they use the same one. Tell them you want them to track the time they use any type of screen at home or work, whether a passive use of the screen such as watching TV or an active use such as playing a video game, composing an email, or reading a work document. Then initiate a family conversation about screen time: turn the tables on them and see what you have discovered. Potential topics could include examining the devices you use, the ratio of game time to work time, passive versus active screen time, and helpful as opposed to distracting screen time.

Respond together to the following questions:

What are the differences between your tracking and that of your parents? How do you explain this difference?

_____

_____

What can you learn from your parents' use of screen time that might help you or them?

_____

_____

How do these observations give you insight into your own video game and screen time?

_____

_____

Try out some ways for joint media engagement where you use screens together.
Consider texting each other, watching a TV show together, playing a video game
together, watching a YouTube video to get you started on a building project, or using
screens for listening to music. Describe what you did here.

_____

_____

Develop and use some family strategies to convert screen time into other healthy
activities. Consider substituting music for TV during dinner, occasional board games
for video games, or a family book club. Describe what you did here.

_____

_____

7   screens and your sleep

Charlie had always been a good student. He also dreamed of being a rock star and knew that his hard work in developing his music skills and at school would pay off in success. He had many interests outside of school: he was a particularly talented singer and songwriter, spent hours practicing the guitar, and had many friends.

But in the past year, he noticed that he wasn't spending nearly as much time developing his musical skills or hanging out with his friends as he used to. Instead of taking guitar and voice lessons, he was spending more time playing League of Legends *late into the night and watching what he called "stupid" YouTube videos about people farting and cats doing tricks.*

Basically, he had substituted screen time for music time, and it was interfering with getting enough sleep. He would wake up tired, often rushing off to school without breakfast or a shower. It hadn't affected his grades yet, but for someone who prided himself on his musical talents and looking good for the girls, he often appeared disheveled in the morning. He had also fallen asleep in class on a few occasions. One of his teachers noticed this and raised concerns that he might be using drugs, resulting in a meeting with the principal and his parents. At that point, he decided he needed to take some action to improve his sleep habits and, in turn, look at his nighttime use of screens.

for you to know

Did you know that teenagers need more sleep than younger children? According to a doctor at the Johns Hopkins Medical School, teenagers need between nine and nine and a half hours of sleep per night, an hour more than ten-year-olds need. The reason is that their brains and bodies are going through growth spurts that require enough sleep to mature at an appropriate pace.

It's very difficult for teenagers to get enough sleep; they tend to stay up later than their younger siblings, and their schools usually begin earlier in the morning than elementary schools. (Interestingly, the historical reason for this is that teens were needed to come home during the daylight and work on the family farm after school.) Recognizing that today's school schedules are not conducive to adequate sleep for teens, the American Academy of Pediatrics, the doctors who set policy for children's health, recently suggested that high schools should start later than elementary schools, allowing teenagers to have more time to sleep in the morning.

Even if you're not playing video games or texting late into the night, screen time can negatively affect your sleep. Many studies have shown that screen time from mobile devices makes sleep less restful. According to a 2018 publication from the Harvard Medical School, the blue light from many screens suppresses the secretion of melatonin, an antioxidant that helps people fall asleep and stay asleep at night. This report also suggests that individuals avoid looking at bright screens two hours prior to bedtime, although other experts suggest that an hour may be adequate.

for you to do

For one week, pay close attention to your use of screens before going to bed. In the morning (not during the middle of the night), take a few minutes to complete the chart that follows. Include at least three days in which you avoid screens for a minimum of an hour or more before going to bed. Then, using a scale of 1 to 4 (1 = poor, 2 = fair, 3 = good, 4 = excellent), compare the quality of your sleep on nights when you used screens up until bedtime to those when you stopped at least sixty minutes earlier. Do this experiment for more than one week to make it more accurate; you can download copies at http://www.newharbinger.com/45519.

Screens and My Sleep Quality

Day	Number of minutes between screen time and bedtime	My sleep quality (1 to 4)
Monday		
Tuesday		
Wednesday		
Thursday		
Friday		
Saturday		
Sunday		

more to do

Your quality of sleep is affected by more than your screen time prior to going to bed. Think about activities that could help you sleep, such as those that might tire your mind or body. Determine what has worked for you in the past, and add other activities as you find them.

Other teens have found that these activities have helped them with sleep:

_____ Exercising for at least an hour to three or more hours prior to bedtime

_____ Reading a hardbound book

_____ Listening to music

_____ Stretching

_____ Doing yoga or meditating

_____ Talking to friends on the phone

_____ Watching a TV program

_____ Using white noise or relaxation music

Other: _____

_____

_____

After you've tried an activity, rate your sleep again using a scale of 1 to 4.

8 do you get distracted by games and screens?

Reice's parents were constantly on her case about how she did her homework. She liked having her cell phone in front of her while doing homework and insisted that social games that don't require constant attention were actually helpful breaks. She was also certain that texting and scrolling her social media did not interfere with getting her work done. She told her parents that she was an excellent multitasker, that she was still an honor student, that she had lots of friends, and that she did not want to miss out on what was going on. She was certain that taking a break to play an occasional online game with her friends didn't distract her from completing her work and insisted that she needed breaks to maintain her energy for schoolwork.

Reice and her parents had so many arguments about this that her parents suggested she might want to think about being a lawyer. Reice didn't like arguing with her parents but was doing well in school, getting her work done, and finding a way to make it less of a grind. She didn't think she would do much better if she put away her phone and games.

for you to know

There's a widespread belief that multitasking can make people more efficient and help them do a few things at the same time. However, neuroscientists have not found this to be true. Rather than allowing us to do things at the same time, the brain stops one task and quickly switches to another and starts again on something else when people multitask. Instead of making us more efficient, multitasking tends to sap people's energy, resulting in their making more mistakes, according to research reported by the American Psychological Association in 2006.

You might not want to believe that attention to texting, technology, and social media interferes with your ability to complete homework or study, but it does. However, there's good news for those of you who feel lost when their phones are out of sight: using a cell phone to listen to music does not interfere with getting your work done!

The impact of multitasking and the distractions it causes are not the same for everyone. Many teens and adults argue that multitasking makes their work more interesting, gives them needed breaks, and may help them learn better. If you find that switching tasks is helpful, you're probably not multitasking but trying to do two things at alternating times. While there is compelling evidence that "interleaved learning," in which students switch back and forth between different subjects, helps with memory and learning, this style of learning involves spending some time with each subject before switching.

for you to do

This self-experiment will help you see how switching between activities (such as studying and playing an online word game with your friends) impacts your efficiency. Recruit a friend or family member to be your "timer" who will help you with this. If you can't find a helper, use the timer on your phone.

On the dotted line write, "I am very good at multitasking." On the next two lines, write out the numbers from 1 to 20 sequentially, with spaces between them but no commas.

....

_____

_____

Check with your timer to see how long it took you to complete the tasks. This typically takes between twenty and thirty seconds.

Now it's time to multitask by going back and forth between the two tasks. Get your "timer" prepared. Start on the dotted line and write the letter _I_, then go to the solid lines and write the number _1_. Continue by alternating from the dotted line to the solid lines, writing one letter or number at a time until you have completed the task.

....

_____

_____

Compare your times. It's likely to have taken you significantly longer to do the second task than the first.

more to do

Try some of the following suggestions for completing your homework and record your experiences. Look at your efficiency in completing your work, any frustration you may have experienced, and your attitude while you were studying.

Do your homework with background music. Set your phone so that you cannot access any games, social media, or the internet.

_____

_____

_____

Do your homework without any electronics in sight. Turn them off, give them to a parent, or put them in a different room. Do this when you have a reading assignment, need to take handwritten notes, or have to do something manually.

_____

_____

_____

Substitute an old-fashioned iPod touch or MP3 player for your cell phone for a day. You would have limited access to the internet and mostly be able to use it for music. Keep notes on whether the change impacted your tendencies to become distracted.

_____

_____

_____

9 how tech tools help with homework and school

Earl is one of the most admired kids in his school. He's a musician and an artist and a wizard at being able to draw what he sees. He is kind, cares about others, and is one of the best listeners among his peers. But if his friends want to find him, they won't see him on Instagram or Snapchat. He doesn't respond to text messages, and they have to call him on his home phone or see him at school, because he doesn't own a smartphone. He and his family are what are described as Luddites—people who choose not to use the latest technologies. Some Luddites struggle to adapt readily to technological change, while others just prefer to use some of the more traditional tools in life.

Earl's computer teacher recently introduced him to computer-aided design (CAD) programs and music production software. He realizes how much these tech tools could enhance his musical and artistic strengths but is concerned about how his parents will feel about his newfound use of technology.

for you to know

More than 80 percent of households in the United States have high-speed internet service. Most of the families who don't have the internet report that they cannot afford it or don't feel as if they need it. Many of those without internet service are elderly people who are not familiar with computers and other technology. In addition, rural areas are less likely to have widely available internet service.

Today, more than 70 percent of students are assigned homework that requires them to be online. More than 80 percent report that they use the internet for research and doing homework. Teachers increasingly use online tools to give homework assignments and instructions so students can look online for assignments or contact fellow students electronically. Doing assignments online also makes it much easier for students to engage in group projects with their peers and allows creation of multimedia projects involving audio, video, and images to go along with text. There is another reason that you might be getting more online homework—multiple choice or other assignments that can be autocorrected make teachers' lives easier.

for you to do

With your teacher's permission, complete a homework assignment without the use of any type of electronics. Choose a small one that won't have a significant impact on your grades, preferably in subjects such as history, English, or social studies, where your primary work will be reading and writing. Find encyclopedias or other books about research topics at home or in a library. Note when the books were published, and consider what information might have changed since that time. Take handwritten notes and then organize them, write down your references, and complete the assignment neatly and on time.

Notice how technology could have made this process easier and perhaps allowed a higher quality result. Consider the time and effort it took to do. Ask older family members what it was like to do their work without technology on a routine basis.

List the positive and negative aspects of doing schoolwork the "old-fashioned" way:

_____

_____

_____

_____

List the positive and negative aspects of doing schoolwork using all the technology at your command:

_____

_____

_____

_____

more to do

Find an assignment that is comparable to the one you completed in the preceding section but was done using technology. Compare the assignments on these dimensions:

	No-tech	High-tech
Number of minutes to complete project (minutes)		
Number of minutes to gather materials		
Number of minutes for transportation		
Number of minutes to handwrite or type assignment		
Number of words in completed assignment		
Depth of information (low to high)		
Timeliness of information (old, recent, current)		
Your engagement in the task (poor, okay, good)		

Now that you've had a chance to compare doing your homework with technology and without, describe your overall impressions and evaluate what works best for you.

_____

_____

_____

_____

_____

Elizabeth's friends and family know her to be a bit scattered. She sometimes forgets her schedule at school and loses jewelry, only to find it weeks later. She once went to a get-together at a friend's house and discovered that she was a week late for the party. She often loses her focus while doing homework on the computer, shifting from working on assignments to searching the internet for interesting information about a favorite entertainer or watching silly YouTube videos.

Elizabeth has always been a bit distractible. Using technology, she can quickly become so immersed in what she is doing that she loses sight of what she had intended to do. One of the more distracting technologies for Elizabeth is semieducational. She enjoys playing online word games and has gone from playing just with her friends to playing with people all over the world. Sometimes these educational word games—which have made her into an impressive Scrabble player—distract her from her homework for hours at a time.

for you to know

Distractibility and inattention are very common. About one out of every ten kids in the United States has been diagnosed with ADHD, and many others have problems staying focused. While ADHD is not caused by video games and technology, experts have questioned whether there is a relationship between increases in diagnoses of ADHD and the use of technology. You might have noticed that it is often easier to pay attention to an exciting video game than it is to many of your teachers. Video games and other technologies are highly stimulating; use sounds, video, and actions to keep you involved; and provide you with immediate feedback. As a result, video games and social media can make the normal pace and activity of your classroom seem boring. Some kids with attention difficulties report that they become overly focused on video games. This type of focus and attention to video games is not unique to people with ADHD, but if you have ADHD or difficulty paying attention, you might notice how easily you can focus on video games and screens.

for you to do

How often do you find yourself distracted from completing your homework or other tasks such as chores as a result of the following circumstances?

	Never	Sometimes	Often	Always
Background noise from the TV				
Conversations between my parents or siblings				
Cell phone alerts from social media				
Checking something on the internet				
Playing a game on my phone				
Receiving a text				
Checking my email				

Which of these is the biggest distractor?

_____

List steps you can take to reduce this distraction.

_____

_____

_____

more to do

These days, it's increasingly important to find ways to reduce distractions. While video games, the internet, and other types of screen time are the focus of this book, there are many other things that can distract you from being efficient at home and school. And perhaps more importantly, these distractions can keep you from being fully focused and mindful of whatever you're doing in the present. Try some of the following strategies, and rate their helpfulness in being more focused and less distracted. Use a scale of 1 to 4 (1 = made it worse, 2 = not helpful, 3 = somewhat helpful, 4 = very helpful).

_____   Give your cell phone to your parent for an hour while doing your homework.

_____   Spend fifteen to twenty minutes meditating, watching a mindfulness video, or doing yoga prior to starting homework.

_____   Wear noise-canceling headphones (with just the noise cancellation operating) while doing your homework.

_____   Wear noise-canceling headphones (listening to music of your choice) while doing your homework.

_____   Wear noise canceling-headphones (listening to classical or nonvocal jazz) while doing your homework.

_____   Sit in isolation with no electronics while doing your homework (for example, in your parent's car, in the bathroom of your home, or in an empty classroom at school).

Which of these approaches did you find to be most helpful, and how can you arrange to use this on a routine basis?

_____

_____

11 video games are more than just fun

Stevie likes to play. His parents enjoy telling stories of how, as a three-year-old, he could sit and play with blocks and LEGOs all day long. He could have fun whether he was at a playground with dozens of other kids or all by himself in the backyard with a few sticks and rocks as his "playmates."

As he's gotten older, Stevie finds that he doesn't like school nearly as much as play, but when he can find a project that involves computers and programming, he really gets into it. In high school, he's also gotten into playing video games. The games he finds to be most fun are those that challenge his brain and skills. He has also learned how to create his own games and has become a wizard at programming. While he's doing fine in school, his parents wish that he would spend a bit more time with schoolwork to prepare for the future, rather than playing games. But Stevie is convinced that his game play and programming are preparing him for the future, and he might just be correct.

for you to know

While psychologists argue about the value of video games for children, they almost all agree that play is the best way for children to learn. Sports, board games, and imaginative play are opportunities to practice skills that children will need when they become adults. Perhaps that's why it's so common for younger children to play games such as house or school. This type of play provides opportunities for exploring and testing their thoughts about the world and helps them understand relationships, cooperation, and problem solving. Competitive games help them learn how to handle success and failure, while strategy games develop their creativity and imagination and help them figure out how to think about the future; for example, learning about investing money for the future when they play Monopoly.

While some educators and psychologists don't view video games as a legitimate form of play, almost all research indicates that having fun playing video games is a healthy part of a child's life. So the next time people tell you that playing video games is a waste of your time, pass on a little knowledge. Tell them that *Minecraft* is used in hundreds of schools to teach math, history, and geology. Let them know that playing video games is a way to practice skills you'll need as an adult; for example, communication, problem solving, and learning from mistakes.

If you have fun playing video games, keep playing; just keep in mind that play is most helpful to you when you don't restrict yourself to video games but also engage in other forms of play.

for you to do

Consider all the play activities you do for fun. Think beyond video games and other media-based play. Do you enjoy sports or board games? Engaging in fantasy and imaginative play or doing puzzles? While some parents, teachers, and kids believe that having fun for fun's sake isn't productive, you now know that play is vital for your development. Start by thinking about how to find video games that are fun and playful.

What is the most fun video game you have ever played?

_____

What genre of video game (role-playing, action, adventure, shooter, sports, strategy, or puzzle game) is your favorite? Why?

_____

_____

Write a list of the specific skills you need to be good at this genre. For example, in strategy games, you need to be flexible in problem solving and use planning and organizational skills.

_____

_____

_____

Demonstrate to your parents how having fun playing video games can actually help you in your daily life. Here's how to do it. Take your list of skills from the previous question, and write how you apply them in the following situations. Make sure to tell your parents about how playing games is helping you learn.

Doing homework

What skill(s) do I use? _____

How I use it (them) _____

_____

Friendships

What skill(s) do I use? _____

How I use it (them) _____

_____

Studying

What skill(s) do I use? _____

How I use it (them) _____

_____

Doing my chores

What skill(s) do I use? _____

How I use it (them) _____

_____

more to do

Playing video games is fun. However, if video games are your only form of play, the only way you have fun, you're limiting yourself. One of the core messages of this book is that overdoing video-game play takes away from other fun activities. While playing on a screen is often the go-to activity for teens and adults, it may be important for you to expand your ways of having fun.

Here are some suggestions from other teenagers; put a check next to any that grab your attention and add others you think of.

☐ Extreme and action sports such as skateboarding, snowboarding, or surfing

☐ Rock climbing in a gym or outdoors

☐ Community service

☐ Road trips with your parents or an older relative

☐ Going to the gym with your friends

☐ Strategy board games such as Catan, chess, Game of Thrones, and Ticket to Ride

☐ Others: _____

☐ Others: _____

Choose one of these activities to do. After you've done it, write down your answers to these questions.

What activity did you choose? _____

In comparison to playing video games:

How much fun was it?

_____

What was the level of interaction with others?

_____

What did I learn?

_____

12 family and video games

Gabe is an eighth-grader who has been feeling down for the past year. His parents divorced when he was twelve, and his father recently moved out of state. He feels sad because he doesn't see his father as often as he would like. It feels a bit strange when they talk on the phone, and Gabe is often unsure what to say about things in his life. He wants to know more about what's going on in his dad's life but doesn't know how to ask.

When his parents were together, Gabe often hung out with his dad, taking out their boat or working in the yard together. His favorite thing to do with his father was to go fishing and then tell stories about the big ones that got away.

One of Gabe's friends, whose parents are also divorced, told him about how much fun he has playing MMOs (massively multiplayer online games) with his father, who also lives out of state. Neither Gabe nor his dad had been an online gamer, but Gabe suggested to his father that they might want to try this together. They began playing online fishing and hunting games together, and while neither of them was particularly good at the games, it gave them an activity to do together and something to talk about. Talking about game-play strategy has led to more comfortable conversation about each other's lives. They've been having so much fun that they've started playing two to three times a week and texting each other between games.

for you to know

Only about 30 percent of parents say they play video games with their kids. More parents report that they watch their kids play video games than report they actually play with their kids. Some parents say they are too busy to play video games, but many more didn't grow up playing video games and aren't very good at them. Sometimes it's just because they haven't tried, but other times their kids (yes, you!) are at fault. They get impatient with parents who don't know the basics about using a controller or strategies required to play a game. Parents have feelings, too, and many don't like being made fun of because of their lack of skill at video-game play.

While it might seem to you that video games have been around forever, the first really popular game system, the Nintendo Entertainment System (NES) was introduced in 1983. So if your parents were born before the early '80s, they may not have been raised on video games. Even more interesting is that video games that allow for multiplayer online use have been available only since about the year 2000 and became popular starting in 2005. If your parents were teenagers prior to 1995, they probably don't have very much experience playing online games.

for you to do

Get your parents to play a video game with you. Remember, you might need to teach them some basics. Have patience. After all, they are old!

To encourage your parents and make playing video games into a fun family experience, here are a few tips to help you find the best games to play with them:

- Ask your parents what types of games and apps they already use.

- Ask your parents about the types of movies they like. (Their answers may give you a clue into game genres—such as action, strategy, puzzle, or sports games—they would like.)

- Select a game you think they would like to play.

- Before playing, consider watching a few Let's Play videos or some live streaming of the game.

Now it's game time.

What were your experiences in playing with your parents?

_____

_____

_____

What do your parents have to say about their game-play experiences with you?

_____

_____

_____

more to do

Try to get your parents interested in playing video games on their own. If they have fun playing, they will better understand your interest in game play. You can use these strategies to help them get started:

- Start with very simple games.

- Teach them about the game before they play. If they feel more knowledgeable or skilled, they are more likely to enjoy their game play.

- Find instructional videos that provide hints for early levels of games. Success breeds success, and your parents are more likely to keep playing if they beat a few levels of a game.

- Choose games that were initially board games (such as chess, Scrabble, Monopoly, Risk) or card games; these often have more levels and feedback in their video-game form.

- If they choose to play with you, let them win!

What seemed most helpful in getting your parents to enjoy their game play?

_____

_____

What else might you try to encourage them to play with you in the future?

_____

_____

13 hanging out with friends

Zander has been playing video games since he was four. As a young child, he liked to play Mario games with his older brother and cousins. He loved the chance to play with the older kids and did not mind losing to them. But when he had the opportunity, he played solo to get better. As he got a bit older, he was able to compete with, and sometimes beat, his relatives.

When Zander entered middle school, his parents let him play online games with his friends. He became an expert in first-person shooters, which he played daily after school with his classmates. He liked hanging out with his friends online but became bored with multiplayer games and began to play only single-player games. He discovered the early games from the Legend of Zelda series. These games were an intense experience for Zander, and once he started, he'd play for hours on end. Playing the game was almost all he could talk and think about. However, he found that his friends were not always interested in hearing more about his game play. After about four months of nonstop Zelda play, he began to feel separated from his friends, missing the banter and competition. He decided to go back to multiplayer games and discovered that the social part of gaming was what he truly enjoyed.

for you to know

Video games have been around for only about fifty years. The earliest games were almost all made for single players, leading to concerns that gamers were isolated from their peers. The first video game, *Spacewar*, was developed by a Massachusetts Institute of Technology student and had two spaceships fighting each other. Many of the games that followed, such as *Pong* (essentially a very simple ping-pong–like game) and *Asteroids*, were primarily one-player games. Early video-game play took place in arcades because the cost and size of computers were not suitable for homes. The first popular home consoles, such as the Magnavox Odyssey and the Coleco Telstar, also had very simple games. The next generation of gaming consoles may sound more familiar to you and included the Nintendo Entertainment System (NES) and the Sega Mark System. At that time, gaming was decades away from being an online experience. If you didn't have a friend or a sibling at home to play alongside, you played alone. Playing video games with others mostly meant taking turns at the console.

Most of the online multiplayer game services did not exist until the 2000s. For example, the original Xbox Live became available in 2002. Before that, if you wanted to play a board or video game with a friend, you had to be in the same space. Playing together meant face-to-face time, which often meant getting a ride to a friend's house, arranging with parents for permission to hang out, and being limited to getting together at specific times.

Online gaming makes playing with your friends a lot easier. Unfortunately, many adults still view teens playing online video games with their friends as isolating. Adults who haven't played an MMO may not realize that you're talking to each other—about the game and everything else—and probably will talk more the next day in school.

for you to do

Online gaming is a social opportunity, particularly when you're doing it with real-life friends. Choose your favorite online multiplayer game and compare it to your favorite single-player game. Where are you more likely to display these behaviors?

	My favorite single-player game:	My favorite multiplayer game:
Laughter		
Focus and concentration		
Easy frustration		
Motivation		
Willingness to make mistakes		
Limiting the amount of game play		
Desire for improvement		
Having fun		
Creativity		

more to do

Vintage video games and consoles have become popular in recent years. Some players like the simplicity and game play of older games. If you haven't played them, give them a try with your friends. Make notes of your experiences in how you learn to play the games, the level of challenge, and how older games differ in the social aspect of playing with friends or observing others playing. (BTW, some of these older games will be familiar to your parents or older relatives, who might want to show you a few tricks.)

Choose at least two of these to play with your friends:

- *Pong*

- *Pac-Man*

- *Asteroids*

- *Space Invaders*

- *Frogger*

- *Donkey Kong*

What were your biggest challenges in playing these games?

_____

_____

_____

What did you learn from your game play?

_____

_____

activity 13 ✳ hanging out with friends

What did you like best about these classic video games?

_____

_____

_____

How does playing these games change how you hang out with your friends?

_____

_____

_____

improving executive functions and problem solving 14

Seventeen-year-old Emma was the valedictorian of her high school class. She planned to attend college and earn a degree in forensic psychology. She had always been fascinated by solving complex problems and able to use her problem-solving skills to do well in school. In her valedictory speech, she attributed much of her success to playing video games. Unsurprisingly, many of the adults in the audience were shocked by this statement until she described what she meant.

Emma reported having played casual video games such as **Diner Dash** *and* **Kingdom Rush** *as a younger child. She described the similarity of these video games to strategy board games, such as Risk and chess. Playing strategy games requires the use of planning and organizational skills. The best players weigh the effectiveness of their tactics and determine what worked and what didn't. She recalled playing more complex strategy games such as* **StarCraft** *and* **Civilization** *as she got older and feeling that this helped her in her math and science classes and in developing better study skills.*

for you to know

Many studies have demonstrated how casual and complex video games can improve problem solving and executive functions. Executive-functioning skills are brain-based skills such as planning, working memory, organization, flexibility, and self-control that help with problem solving and setting and achieving goals. When you plan how to complete a class project, organize your notes, or manage your time so you can get your homework done *and* still hang out with your friends, you're using your executive-functioning skills.

Many video games require the use of planning skills, flexibility, and thinking before acting. As a result, players often practice these executive-functioning and problem-solving skills in their game play. Most of the studies suggest that video-game play alone has only a limited impact on improving these skills in the real world. However, experts indicate that gamers who actively think about the strategies they are using in a game or talk to their peers about game play are better able to recognize how executive-functioning skills can be applied to the real world.

for you to do

Start thinking about your favorite games. They are probably not the ones that are easiest to beat or last for only a few minutes. Most kids tell us that they love involved games that keep their brains engaged and on edge. They like games that require them to focus, remember what has worked (or not worked) in earlier parts of the game, and consider what other players might be thinking. These skills, such as organization, flexibility, and time management are all considered to be executive functions.

On a scale from 1 (not at all) to 10 (a lot), rate how much playing video games has helped you better understand and use these executive-functioning skills.

Planning	1	2	3	4	5	6	7	8	9	10
Working memory	1	2	3	4	5	6	7	8	9	10
Organization	1	2	3	4	5	6	7	8	9	10
Flexibility	1	2	3	4	5	6	7	8	9	10
Self-control	1	2	3	4	5	6	7	8	9	10
Time management	1	2	3	4	5	6	7	8	9	10

more to do

Researchers have discovered what you already know: real-world improvement in problem-solving and executive-functioning skills requires that you do more than just play a video game. (Wouldn't it be great if playing a few hours of video games a day made you an expert at organization, time management, and self-control?)

To make popular video games a tool that improves your executive functions, you'll need to pay close attention, think a lot, and use game-based skills in the real world. Here are the steps we suggest:

1. DETECT, or identify, the skills you're using.

2. REFLECT, or think about, how each skill helps in game play and how it might help in the real world.

3. CONNECT, or practice, using the skills in as many situations possible.

You can improve your ability to translate game-based learning into real-world skills by watching others play the same game, talking to your friends about strategies they use in their game play, and following these three simple steps: detect, reflect, and connect.

Pick one of your favorite puzzle, strategy, or adventure games. These games are often the best for using executive-functioning skills. Consider how you're using problem-solving and executive-functioning skills.

Name of the game: _____

Executive functions used in the game: _____

DETECT: Identify where you used these skills in the game.

_____

_____

_____

REFLECT: Recognize and describe how these skills helped you in the game and how they could help you in the real world.

_____

_____

_____

CONNECT: Find an activity where you can practice the skills you used in the game and apply them. Write down the activity, and describe how you used the skills.

_____

_____

_____

CONNECT again, using a different activity.

_____

_____

_____

promoting creativity with games and apps 15

Miguel is a tenth-grader with big ideas about the world. He likes to talk about politics, environmental issues, music, and his latest project. He also enjoys sports but sometimes seems to mix up the rules of basketball with hockey. Miguel is an artist but not in the conventional sense of the word. He likes to design, create, and build things. From the time he was a child, he has constructed huge forts in his backyard. He drew up designs for his first treehouse at the age of ten. He was always making up plans for homes and buildings on paper, but then discovered a few apps to help him expand his ideas.

His creativity and inventiveness became more evident when he started playing sandbox video games such as Minecraft *and* Fortnite. *He is able to create replicas of buildings from his neighborhood as well as famous buildings from history. His friends are amazed by his elaborate online constructions and are certain he has a career in architecture. Miguel has found that the openness of sandbox games allows his creativity to flourish and inspires him to take artistic risks that he might not do with more concrete projects.*

for you to know

One of the common criticisms of video-game play is that it makes children less creative. Old-school educators believe that unstructured play, in which kids are left to play with simple household items—such as boxes, pencils, and tape—fosters more creativity than modern technological tools and video games. These critics believe that less complex toys and games are better for developing children's imaginations.

Studies suggest that the opposite is true. As reported by Sandra Russ and Jessica Dillon of Case Western Reserve University, researchers who have been studying children's play over the last four decades have found that kids growing up in the twenty-first century are far more creative than kids from the twentieth century. This creativity is due to all the incredible things that kids are able to do with technology. High-tech toys have more options in how to play with them. For example, because old-style wooden blocks are all more or less the same, children are limited in how they can use them. More recent versions of blocks, such as LEGO or K'NEX, are varied in size, shape, color, and function, so they can be made into an unlimited number of variations. While some modern toys and video games have a structured, noncreative component (think about rigidly following the instructions for a LEGO Star Wars figure), most have many ways to use them. Similarly, popular board games have a single platform and, most often, only one level for play, while the same game in a video game format can have multiple levels, designs, and challenges.

for you to do

Think about the many ways you can be creative while using technology. Even something as common as using the camera on your phone (where you can take, review, combine, and alter thousands of pictures in real time) facilitates a whole new form for creative thinking and products. YouTube has fostered creativity in the millions of contributors who make videos. Or consider creative business models and ideas that support many YouTubers. In video games, players commonly create their own avatars, develop their own quests, or construct their own worlds.

In this activity, you'll use your device and document how you use your creative abilities. Choose a game, app, or other technology, and do something you have never done before. Here are some ideas for a creative tech or video game activity. Feel free to add your own.

- Construct something in a sandbox game.

- Create a music video.

- Make a website.

- Create a song or music to share with others.

- Make up an entirely new avatar in a game you have played.

- Other: _____

- _____

What tech tool did you use? _____

What did you do?

_____

_____

How were you creative?

_____

_____

How did your idea turn out?

_____

_____

What might you do differently next time?

_____

_____

more to do

Learn how to use your creativity with video games and technology to make a great class presentation. Before you do your next class presentation, ask your parents about class presentations they made in high school. Most likely, they'll tell you they made posters on large pieces of cardboard and read prepared speeches. That would be considered boring today, when you can show videos, play music, use PowerPoints, or play an online game as part of a class presentation.

Consider some of the following ways to use tech creatively in your next class presentation.

- Play a video game on a smartboard that demonstrates a scientific or mathematical principle or is set in a historical or geographical location.

- Use your classmates' cell phones to poll them in a survey you have created.

- Create a video as part of your presentation.

- Put your entire presentation online into a website or using social media so others can view and comment on it.

How did using technology creatively enhance your presentation?

_____

_____

In what ways did technology take away from your main points?

_____

_____

What old-school tools were helpful in your presentation?

_____

_____

How do you think your use of video games and technology made learning more fun and engaging for your classmates?

_____

_____

16 stress and relaxation

Dom is a hard worker and a straight A student who is determined to go to medical school. He has a few jobs after school, including owning a landscaping business with his best friend. His motto is "Do, do, do." He needs to keep busy; he's always moving and never wanting to stop doing things, and sometimes finds it hard to relax.

Playing video games is the one activity during which Dom can relax and stop moving. Interestingly, he likes playing sports video games in which the players are constantly moving. His favorites are soccer and basketball games, two sports he likes to play in real life but doesn't show a lot of talent for. While Dom has become very skilled at these video games, he isn't very competitive when he plays, focusing instead on having fun, trying out new moves, and relaxing.

for you to know

Among the most common reasons teenagers identify for playing video games are to relax and reduce stress. Many teens find that playing video games helps them get away from the demands of school and extracurricular activities. Video games allow them to be fully absorbed in an activity and not think so much about everything else that's going on. Far more than a waste of time, this can be an opportunity to recharge their batteries. Unfortunately, some adults think that relaxing while playing a video game is somehow less valuable than relaxing while watching a movie or a football game on TV.

There is strong scientific evidence supporting video-game play as a tool for stress management. At the same time, you need to know that gaming can also sometimes cause stress. If you're a competitive gamer or just hate to lose, you may experience frustration and anxiety about your performance. If you spend too much time playing, stress is almost sure to follow; you may fall behind in school, have your parents on your case, or cut back on activities that are healthy for you—and maybe even all three. It is probably best if you have a few different activities that help you relax beyond video games. And don't forget, taking time for destressing with play that doesn't involve video games is important for your physical and mental health. Many studies describe how human play is related to mental and physical health and can improve productivity at work and school. Taking breaks or vacations from work has also been found to improve creativity and perspective taking.

for you to do

One of the easiest ways to reduce your stress level is to do more relaxing activities on a regular basis. If that method happens to be video-game play, go for it, but make sure you do other things as well. Note how much stress you experience in the following activities.

	None	Occasional	Frequent	Constant
Being at school				
Doing homework				
Getting up in the morning to go to school				
Getting along with your friends				
Handling social media				
Exercising				
Playing video games				
Going for a walk				
Shopping				
Participating in extracurricular activities				
Being with family				

If more than six of these activities are sources of frequent or constant stress, it's time to make some changes. Talk to your parents, friends, or school counselors to find ways to reduce your stress.

more to do

Now that you have identified activities that are causing you stress, you can do something to help. Choose two of these healthy activities to reduce your stress in an area you identified above. If you choose a technology-based activity, also select a nontech activity. These activities have been suggested because they are easy to do on a regular basis. Keep track of how often you do them in the next week, and determine if they are helping to reduce your stress.

- Exercise outdoors.

- Go to a gym.

- Meditate or do mindfulness training.

- Play a video game with your friends.

- Play a one-person video game.

- Read a book of your choosing.

- Go for a hike or walk.

- Hang out with friends and play a board game.

- Play with your pet.

- Hang out with your friends in person.

- Sit outdoors and do nothing for twenty to thirty minutes.

Which activities did you choose?

_____

_____

How did one week of each activity impact your stress level?

_____

_____

What could you do to reduce your stress even more?

_____

_____

What (if any) other benefits of reducing stress did you notice; for example, better focus, sleep, or memory?

_____

_____

developing and expanding interests 17

Scott is an eleventh-grader who considers himself a musician. He's been taking lessons since he was thirteen and has developed his expertise by practicing on a daily basis. Unlike some of his friends, who spend hours trying to copy lead guitar solos from their favorite songs, Scott is focused on developing the core skills of musicianship.

He has also become interested in how digital electronics could enhance his music. He has become an expert in using GarageBand to create music and has learned about more sophisticated tools for producing music. One of his friends is into making videos and has begun to produce music videos of Scott's band; one video has even gone viral. Scott has expanded his expertise with music games and technology to making more videos and developing a large online following for his band.

for you to know

People are not born with intense interests or passions but develop them through exposure and opportunity. Fifty years ago, it would have been impossible to have a passion for playing video games, as they did not exist, but now it's very common. Your interests are likely to be influenced by what your family and friends enjoy. Because of new technologies, there are now many more opportunities to notice what others in your broader community are doing. You may learn more about what others enjoy through social media, the internet, and other screen-based technologies that have made the world seem smaller. These factors make it both easier and harder to have a passion: easier because you might more readily find an interest that captures your fancy, harder because there are too many choices.

Experts on future trends suggest that you're likely to have as many as eight different types of jobs throughout your lifetime. If this is the case, having just a single passion may not serve you well. While many speakers at high school and college graduations encourage students to follow their passions, psychologists have found that *developing* your passions—trying things and expanding interests—may be a better path.

For example, if you love video games and dream about a career as a professional gamer, try to expand your interests to all things involving video games and technology. The number of people who earn a living as a professional gamer is very limited, but there are countless others in related industries such as app development, website creation, video marketing and publicity, movies and TV production, or computer programming.

for you to do

If you're reading this book, it's likely you have some passion for playing video games and using other technologies. We want to help you explore how your excitement with gaming might also be a tool for finding other passions and interests. Here are some thought experiments to help:

What do you like to do for more than an hour at a time?

_____

_____

What do you think about when you're relaxed or daydreaming?

_____

_____

Picture yourself as an adult with a job. What do you see?

_____

_____

What are your favorite subjects at school?

_____

_____

What are your favorite current activities that do not use technology?

_____

_____

Think about the adults in your life you most admire. What are their passions, and what do they do for work and fun?

_____

_____

Go online and learn more about the jobs most likely to be available between now and 2030. Job sites such as LinkedIn or futurist blogs are good places to search. What strikes your interest?

_____

_____

more to do

Play a video game intensively for one week that is connected to an area of personal interest. Remember, passions are developed through activity and opportunity. Choose one of the *content* categories listed below, such as architecture or history, or choose your own and play a related game. The goal of this exercise is to take an existing interest and develop it through playing video games.

- Architecture and construction (*Minecraft*)

- History (*Total War: Shogun 2*, Civilization series, *Red Dead Redemption 2*)

- Military history (Original *Call of Duty*)

- Agriculture and gardening (*Farmville*)

- Sports (*FIFA 20, NBA 2K20*)

Follow up on the game content by reading more about it—watching documentaries, videos, or movies; listening to podcasts; or just talking with your friends or family about this interest.

What did you learn about this area of interest?

_____

_____

_____

How did your game play impact your interest?

_____

_____

_____

What other steps could you take to nurture this interest?

_____

_____

_____

18 learning more about the world

Harry is a high school senior who has a passion for traveling and learning about other countries. He accidentally discovered his skills at learning languages a few years earlier. After arguing with his parents for a number of years, he finally received permission to play the newest Call of Duty *game and found himself regularly playing in a group of kids from Canada who spoke French. He had been taking French in high school and was an excellent student, but certainly not the best in his class. However, he needed to speak French when playing with his Canadian peers and eventually became adept at conversational French so he could work with his teammates. Playing most afternoons for a few months expanded his French vocabulary dramatically. Without any conscious effort, he had become almost fluent in French.*

As a result of his newfound expertise, he was nominated by his French teachers for a statewide award in foreign languages that he later won. While he did not start his Call of Duty *play as an intentional effort to help him at school, game play has helped him become fluent in French and fostered his interests in other cultures and travel.*

for you to know

In the 1980s, video game companies began publishing edutainment games; a few of these, including *Where in the World Is Carmen Sandiego?* and *Oregon Trail*, became best sellers. Because video games are so much fun, game companies thought they could easily apply game mechanics (the structure and methods that games use to keep you involved) to teach academics. However, most of you are not playing video games to improve your school skills, and most video games are not made with this intention. Game publishers know that academic games are not big sellers. Most of the educational games and apps that are fun are made for younger kids.

In the past decade, there has been a movement to create fun, educational games for teens. These games are not about traditional school topics but for learning about issues such as the environment, poverty, mental health, government, and nutrition. Most of these games are shorter, casual games that are often created by small, independent publishers. Organizations such as Games for Change and iThrive Games are supporting game publishers in the creation of engaging learning games. These and other organizations are starting to recognize the power of video games for teaching academic, empowerment, and self-help skills.

for you to do

It's widely accepted that you can learn and expand your knowledge by reading works of fiction and nonfiction, watching a movie or documentary, or listening to a lecture. Why can't you learn from video-game play? Of course you can! While games set in different countries and time eras may not be 100 percent factual, most are accurate enough to spark your interest, and you can play video games that educate you about a specific topic of importance to you.

These organizations address social and educational issues in the games they produce or recommend:

- MIT Game Lab

- Games for Change

- iThrive Games

- Games and Learning Society

Do some research on each of these organizations to see how they use games to educate.

Which organization was of most interest to you? _____

Describe their mission and how effectively you think their use of games helps them accomplish it.

_____

_____

_____

Choose a game from this organization to play. After you've played it, rate it on a scale from 1 (not at all) to 10 (a lot):

Was it educational?	1	2	3	4	5	6	7	8	9	10
Was it well-made?	1	2	3	4	5	6	7	8	9	10
Did it make you think?	1	2	3	4	5	6	7	8	9	10
Did it encourage you to talk to others?	1	2	3	4	5	6	7	8	9	10

more to do

You can use video games as a type of screen-based tour to educate yourself about different cultures. By searching online, you'll find interesting games set in countries such as China, Japan, Russia, the Middle East, and Africa.

Select a country that interests you. As you play, pay attention to things that are portrayed as being different in that country compared to your own: architecture, buildings, stadiums, language, expressions, activities, and food.

Keeping in mind that representations of other countries in video games are likely to be exaggerated and inaccurate, use other screen-based tools (websites, movies, Google maps, documentaries, and internet searches) to learn more and determine how accurately the game portrays it.

What country did you select? _____

What did you learn about this country in game play?

_____

_____

What more would you like to learn about this country?

_____

_____

What was the most interesting difference between the video-game portrayal and your internet research on this country?

_____

_____

What is the most interesting difference between your country and the one you explored?

_____

_____

19 can video games make you more efficient?

Jimmy is super quick at water polo and a fast-moving, left-handed basketball player with an uncanny shot, but he tends to do things very slowly when it comes to getting ready to go places with his friends, completing an assignment for school, or reading a book. His friends always have to wait for him when they go out. His parents have learned to give him many warnings to get ready for school or when they are going out for a family activity. When he is not late for something, everyone is surprised.

He has also noticed that it takes him longer to complete tests and assignments in school than it does his friends. When given enough time, he's usually an A student, but he struggles to get timed tests and classroom writing assignments done promptly.

Jimmy recently began playing some action video games that require him to think quickly, react to the on-screen activity, and make decisions without dwelling on them. At first, he wasn't successful in these games because of his slow decision making. But as he kept playing them, he got better at reacting quickly and more decisively. At the same time, he noticed that he was getting his homework done more quickly than he had in the past. He wonders whether his improved speed at schoolwork is because he wants to have time to play video games or if the games themselves have helped him move faster at other activities.

for you to know

There is strong evidence that playing certain types of action video games can make you do things faster. Improving your speed of processing helps you take in information more quickly, make a decision about what to do with this information, and then act on that decision. While it sounds complicated, it's really not. Some video games require that you think or act quickly. Studies have shown how action games can train your brain and help you learn what you need to pay attention to and what you can ignore. Other studies have demonstrated that playing fast-moving video games can help with reading more fluently.

for you to do

Some kids tend to do things slowly. Psychologists can measure this attribute and have defined it as "slow processing speed." Most kids with slow processing speed are excellent learners but need more time to complete their schoolwork. If you find getting things done in a timely fashion to be difficult, it may be helpful to determine the specific area where you slow down.

Using the columns labeled Week 1, check how often the following concerns relate to you.

	Never		Sometimes		Often	
	Week 1	Week 2	Week 1	Week 2	Week 1	Week 2
It takes too long to do reading assignments.						
I'm always late to see my friends.						
It's difficult for me to wake up and get moving in the morning.						
I take forever to do writing assignments.						
It takes me longer than my friends to do homework.						

If you checked "sometimes" or "often" to four or more of these areas, consider a course of action video-game "treatment." Sounds like fun, right?

Choose an action video such as a *Call of Duty* game, *Fortnite*, a Batman game, or a *Red Dead Redemption* game. Play it for an hour a day for one week, and then complete the checklist again, using the columns labeled Week 2. See if you notice any improvement in your speed of processing. It's unlikely that you'll discover immediate or vast improvement; in the studies, subjects played for at least one month and showed only small improvements. But it would be a fun experiment! You might see more direct improvement using apps and technologies in the More to Do section.

more to do

Wouldn't it be great if playing video games made it easier to do your homework in half the time it normally takes? Sorry, but it doesn't work like that. While the evidence suggests that certain types of action video games might help you process information more quickly, the improvements are still small. However, there are many great apps and technology tools that could help you with going faster. Some apps work by supporting weaker skills, others by making you more aware of time or improving your efficiency. Look through this list of areas where you might like to go faster, and try some of the apps and technologies that are suggested.

- *Getting homework done.* Consider timer apps such as 30/30, Hatch-Stay Focused, or other tools, such as your clock/alarms on your cell phone, that help you monitor your time and attention.

- *Reading faster.* Consider listening to audio books rather than reading. Try a text-to-speech app. Play a party game such as *Rayman Raving Rabbids*.

- *Being on time.* Use Google Calendar or another app on your phone that gives you alerts. Arrange with friends and family to send you text alerts to be ready.

- *Writing faster.* Stop handwriting and use technology. Become an expert typist through practice. Find apps and casual games that promote typing speed. Find the best type of keyboard that works for you. Alternatively, learn dictation skills.

Which area did you work on?

_____

Write about any improvement you saw.

_____

_____

How did the technology or app help you?

_____

_____

What can you do to keep improving your speed of processing?

_____

_____

What other tools and technologies might help you?

_____

_____

20 exercise and games

Cooper is a rising senior at a large suburban high school. As an all-around athlete with an incredible pitching arm, he is being recruited by several high-profile colleges. After he experienced a few injuries while running on the bumpy turf at his school, he began looking for a new way to stay in shape.

Cooper is also a technology geek and is often the first in his class to try new technology. Recently, he found some virtual reality (VR) programs for exercise where he rides his exercise bike through national parks and along the ocean. He's now in the best shape of his life. In his exercise regimen, he plays video games that use VR for sports such as dodgeball, boxing, and martial arts. Cooper has found VR exercise to be very engaging and reports he's never had such great workouts. He's trying to get other members of his baseball team to join him in his workouts.

for you to know

Movement-based video games have been demonstrated to burn calories in a similar fashion to typical exercise. Of course, this requires that people do more than simply move their arms or wrists. The earliest systems designed for active and movement-based video-game play were the Nintendo Wii systems. While first used by children, over time they became a major form of exercise for the elderly.

VR movement-based video games offer a more intense exercise experience. Some games have you boxing against an opponent, others using your arm as a sword to slice objects approaching you. VR games are becoming more adaptable to an individual's performance and interests so that exercise does not become boring.

for you to do

Determine how much exercise you can get from playing video games and compare this to traditional exercise. You'll need to use a fitness tracker in order to do this. You may also be able to use an app on your phone to track your fitness.

Find something simple to measure, such as walking for an hour, going for a thirty- to forty-five-minute bike ride, or spending half an hour doing calisthenics.

Next, try an "exergame" such as a sports or a movement-based fighting game that requires actual movement on your part. Use your fitness tracker to see how many steps you took and how many calories you burned.

Which method worked best?

_____

Describe your motivation for continuing your exercise with each method.

_____

_____

How could you increase your exercise with video games?

_____

_____

Which did you like most, and why?

_____

_____

more to do

Pay attention to whether games and technology improve or increase your exercise. Do one full week of game-based or tech-encouraged exercise. Track your time, calories, and steps with a fitness tracker. If you can access a quality VR headset, try it with games such as *Beat Saber* or *Sparc*. If not, find a more traditional gaming system and do a dance game. If gaming is unavailable, use a screen-based technology such as listening to an audiobook or podcast while running, or watching TV while on an exercise bike.

Notice whether using a fitness tracker helps you exercise more, and whether you work out any harder or for a longer period of time with tech tools.

What did you find?

_____

_____

_____

We strongly encourage you to think about other ways you could use game play and screen time to engage in more physical exercise. Exercise can become somewhat boring or repetitive for many people. One of the great advantages of screen-based technologies is their changing nature. Use them to benefit your physical and mental health.

can competitive video games help your future? 21

Max has always been a competitor. Whether it was playing basketball against his older brother or cousins or trying to get the best grade in his class, he has used competition for self-improvement. When he started high school, his competitive drive took him from the playing field to the computer screen.

During his freshman year in high school, Max began playing different games, including Overwatch, League of Legends, and Rocket League. Soon he was invited to be on a competitive League of Legends team. His teammates were entering tournaments on a regular basis and wanted to play and practice every day. Max began to wonder about how much time his teammates spent on schoolwork and if they had any other interests besides League of Legends. Some even talked about becoming professional gamers. However, Max recognized that professional gaming was a long shot, and he had plans to go to college for business. After a long weekend tournament, Max decided that he was spending too much of his time and energy on esports and decided to leave his team so he could have more time for his friends and schoolwork.

for you to know

Technically speaking, esports involve competition while playing video games. While online esports games such as *Dota 2*, *Hearthstone*, *Fortnite*, and *League of Legends* are examples of modern esports, the original esports were any video games that could be played competitively. The first official video-game competition occurred at Stanford University in October 1972 in a game called *Spacewar*. In the 1980s, the *Space Invaders* championship attracted over ten thousand players in an esports competition. At that time, all the play needed to occur face-to-face, often with hundreds of participants in regional competitions. Esports now connect gamers to the internet. Not only can you play against other people all over the world, but you also don't need to be in the same location as your teammates.

Since about 2010, large tournaments have offered millions of dollars in prize money. Esports have drawn large crowds of people in stadiums as well, with live streaming to watch the competitions. The popularity of esports has made it possible for some gamers to become professionals. Pro gamers have the potential to earn a substantial income by playing video games. However, the best estimates suggest that only one out of every ten thousand video-game players become professional, which is much lower than the odds of becoming a professional football player. In addition, the career life of a professional gamer is often very short, and the income of most professional gamers is generally limited.

This is not to say that an interest in gaming and technology may not be a fantastic opportunity for your professional life. There are many opportunities in game development, music, and art related to video games and in the business aspects of games and technology. Pro gamers have used YouTube and other media tools to earn a very good living playing video games. However, before you decide that becoming a professional gamer is your destiny, be sure to consider how difficult a path this may be to follow.

for you to do

Learn about professional gamers and how they became successful. Examine their practice habits and training. You'll find that many pros incorporate physical and mental exercise into their regimens. Research professional salaries for esports. Go online to explore professional gaming communities to learn about the lives of gamers beyond their chosen esports. To get the inside story about the latest changes in the gaming industry and professional gamers, go online and check out Kotaku, Polygon, and Major League Gaming.

Follow the lives of gamers on Instagram, Twitter, or other social media. Research up-and-coming professional gamers who have a smaller following, and reach out to them to learn how they developed the expertise to go pro.

Asking these questions may make gamers more open to talking to you:

- What were your favorite games growing up?

- How much did you play when you were in elementary, middle, and high school?

- How has your game play affected you in school? In social relationships? With your family?

- What have been your best and worst experiences in playing video games?

more to do

If you're interested in a career involving video gaming, don't limit yourself to becoming a professional gamer. Esports teams already exist and are growing dramatically. Learning more about the business of professional sports teams can help you see what your love of esports might become. The chart that follows lists departments that are typically found in a traditional sports team, as well as the usual responsibilities managed by those departments.

Some of these responsibilities will exist in both traditional and esports teams; other won't. For example, an esports team would be seeking sponsors and selecting players but wouldn't sell tickets or need to maintain a practice facility. Use your knowledge and interest in video games and esports to describe what these departments might be responsible for on an esports teams.

Typical sports team departments	Responsibilities on a traditional team	Responsibilities on an esports team
Marketing	Social media, publicity, public relations	
Operations	Arranging matches, transportation, travel	
Research	Analytics, data collection, new business	
Finance	Salaries, ticket pricing, profitability, getting sponsors	
Human resources	Hiring, firing, creating teamwork	
Manager/coaches	Selection of players, team morale, arranging practices	
Facilities	Equipment, practice facility	
Medical/health	Exercise, mental health, medical issues	
Other:		

When you're done, write about the type of role you might be best suited for.

_____

_____

_____

_____

_____

22 how much time do you spend with screens?

Marc was an excellent athlete, a left hander whose fast hands served him well on the baseball field and basketball and tennis courts. He found out that his fast hands and reflexes were also great tools for playing video games. He and a few of his athlete friends really enjoyed playing esports due to the competitive nature of playing against other teams.

But Marc's parents had always been anti-video–game play. In fact, part of why he played so many sports was a result of his parents' efforts to keep him away from screens. From the time he was young, they had limited how much time he was allowed to play video games or be on the computer. As he got older and performed well in school—he was an honor-roll student in his sophomore year—his parents set fewer limits on him. He was usually too busy with sports to spend much time playing video games—until he became a competitive esports player. For the first time, discussions about screen time with his parents became arguments. Rather than fight with his parents about his gaming, he began monitoring the amount of time he was playing esports. He used a screen tracking app and found that he didn't play for very long on school days but did little else besides play on his Overwatch *and* League of Legends *teams on weekends.*

for you to know

There are many parental control devices available for computers, tablets, and phones designed to limit how much kids play video games and engage with social media. Most of these tools provide information to parents but not to kids and can be a source of arguments between them. Many kids view these parental control tools as another video game—something to beat! Until recently, most of the screen-monitoring tools have been intended for control, rather than providing information about the type and amount of screen use.

In 2017, Apple and Google introduced programs to monitor the amount and type of screen time, including video games, social media, and other apps. Apple's Screen Time and Google's Family Link are available on all devices and provide an excellent source of information that teenagers and adults can use to examine their screen time. They are easy to set up and use and present a useful picture of how you spend your time with technology.

for you to do

Using Apple's Screen Time or Google's Family Link, monitor your screen time. Set up the app to track your video games, social media, and other screen-based activities. It would also be helpful to learn some of the technical aspects of using these tools. Once you learn how to use them properly, you should be able to monitor all the time you spend on your phone, computer, or tablet and how much time you spend listening to music or text messaging.

Here's what to do:

1. Install a screen-time monitor. (Screen Time is already on new Apple devices. You may need to download Android's Family Link, which is not as user-friendly for self-monitoring.)

2. Watch a YouTube video or play with the app to learn the basics.

3. For one week, use it for monitoring, not limiting, your screen and video-game time. Measure what you're doing, preferably on your own and not with parental oversight. The goal is not to stop your game play or screen time but to be aware of what you're doing.

What was the most interesting finding?

_____

_____

Did you spend more, less, or about the amount of time you expected on games and screen time?

_____

_____

What would you like to change, and why?

_____

_____

What steps do you need to take in order to make the changes?

_____

_____

more to do

Now it's time to involve your parents, and not just to show what you're doing. Get them to monitor their own screen and video time for one week. Also have them monitor TV time that is not accounted for by Apple's Screen Time and Google's Family Link. Most likely, you'll need to teach them how to use these apps. Do not hold back! This activity is designed to give a realistic view of what you and your parents are doing with your devices.

Next, ask your parents these questions about their screen-time use and compare your results:

What was the most interesting finding?

_____

_____

Did you spend more, less, or about the amount of time you expected on games and screen time?

_____

_____

What would you like to change, and why?

_____

_____

What steps do you need to take in order to make the changes?

_____

_____

23 a world without technology

Arn is entering middle school. Both of his parents work for internet-based companies and were among the first generation of gamers from the 1990s. They still play video games occasionally and spend much of their free time on their cell phones and other screens. His siblings are also into video games, and one of his sisters is pursuing a career in virtual reality gaming. But Arn is old-fashioned. He studies the Bible, likes to read, spends hours at school, and enjoys hiking and biking. His friends are always trying to get him to play video games with them and are amazed at his lack of interest.

Their amazement is even greater because his parents don't care how much he or his siblings play video games or use their screen time. Many of his friends report that their parents don't like them playing video games, and they complain about the restrictions their parents impose on them. Arn wishes that his parents would set screen-time limits on his siblings. He has become concerned that his family spends too much time with screens and not enough doing other things. He would like to travel more with his family, go camping, and explore nature, but they need to be wired at all times. He has tried to get them away from their screens and engaged in some of these activities but hasn't had much success.

for you to know

The technologies, video games, and screens that are everywhere today are mostly inventions of the past fifteen to twenty years. The iPhone (the first internet-connected smartphone that did more than text and make phone calls) was introduced in 2007. iPads and most other tablets weren't marketed until around 2010. Although laptops were introduced around 1980, they didn't become common until the mid '90s.

Perhaps the most remarkable invention is the internet. While technically developed in the 1980s, the internet did not become widely used until 2000, and its reach and speed have increased dramatically in the last twenty years. In 2000, about a half billion people in the world had some limited access to it, while today, close to four billion do. Its speed is estimated to be a hundred times faster than it was in the early 2000s. To give you some perspective, streaming video on Netflix was barely watchable when it was introduced in 2007 due to slow internet speed. Now it's doubtful that you ever think about the streaming speed in your online gaming or other activities.

for you to do

Choose a day or, if you're feeling brave, a week to eliminate the use of twenty-first-century electronic devices, including video games, apps, cell phones, cable TV, and the internet (with an exception for using your phone to make or receive phone calls). Watch only the major TV networks. If you need to play video games, do so only on a console with a disk. Don't use the internet when you're on the computer. Use software such as Microsoft Word for writing documents, or other software that is not internet-based. Study at the library or take out books rather than going online to do your research. Read bound books, not e-books.. Make all these changes and others to go back in time. The premise of this exercise is to help you see how life was only twenty years ago.

activity 23 ✱ a world without technology

Answer the following questions:

What did you miss most when you went back in time?

_____

_____

Did you cheat? Why or why not?

_____

_____

What did you need to do differently because of the lack of internet access?

_____

_____

How did it change your efficiency at being able to complete tasks or do things?

_____

_____

What did you do to fill in your time when you might typically have used the internet, played video games, or gone on social media?

_____

_____

more to do

Using the library to do research on your destination, plan a one- or two-day family trip during which you'll all use only old-fashioned technology. For example, you could go to an isolated beach where there is no cell service, or climb a mountain, restricting your cell phone use only for safety.

On the way to your destination, don't use your cell phone, watch videos, use a tablet, or listen to satellite radio. Encourage your parents to pay for everything in cash rather than with a credit card. Use a paper map rather than GPS. Make note of other ways you might use technology without a second thought, but try to do this adventure with only the basics.

Describe the nontech tools and strategies you used for each part of your adventure.

Planning the trip

_____

_____

Learning about the destination

_____

_____

Transportation

_____

_____

Paying for the trip

_____

_____

Entertainment during the trip

_____

_____

Communicating with others

_____

_____

Making any reservations or getting tickets

_____

_____

Directions from place to place

_____

_____

Write about the pros and cons of using technology to help you on your adventure.

What did you like about the nontech approach?

_____

_____

_____

What did you not like?

_____

_____

_____

Ask your parents to tell you more about what similar experiences were like for them when they were younger. Even better, ask your grandparents or other older relatives to do the same. What did you learn?

_____

_____

_____

24 when you can't stop looking at screens

Bek loves cars. When he was younger, he had a collection of more than five hundred Matchbox cars, including about a hundred of his favorite Mercedes-Benzes, BMWs, and other German cars. By the age of ten, he could and would tell anyone within earshot everything they ever wanted to know about each and every Mercedes-Benz model built since 1960.

As he got older, he transferred his love of automobiles to playing racing video games. He could not get enough of racing games such as Mario Kart *or* Need for Speed. *Beyond playing racing games, he spent almost all his time browsing the internet for deals on cars, gathering information about new models, and engaging in chats about old Mercedes-Benz models. As soon as he turned sixteen, he bought his first car, a twenty-year-old Mercedes diesel. However, he was frustrated that he didn't have time to work on his car because he couldn't separate himself from his screen-time activities. He began to wonder if there was something wrong with him or if the lure of video games and the internet was just too powerful.*

for you to know

Do you think it's a coincidence that ads pop up on virtually every screen you open? Have you noticed that fast-moving online games restart as soon as you finish a game? Do you find it odd that there is product placement of things you might buy in many of the video games?

Technology can be designed to make it addicting and difficult to ignore. Experts who study tech companies have identified common hooks to get you engaged, including creating small, reachable goals and then getting immediate feedback. Other hooks include making observable progress to encourage a player's desire to do a little more, having ongoing but achievable challenges, and providing uncertainty so you don't want to miss out.

None of these things happen by accident. The longer you stay on a screen playing a video game, looking up something for school, or engaging with your social media feed, the more opportunity there is for commercial success on the part of technology companies. They want you to stay and buy things. And they are *really, really smart* at doing this.

for you to do

The next two activities are designed to contrast your full engagement with technology with an effort to detach and disconnect. First, go to an online game site. Choose either short casual games on a site such as Addicting Games, Kongregate, or Armor games, or consider Steam or the Epic Games Store if you'd rather try a more involved game and search for a free game. While the primary goal of this activity is to notice how games keep you engaged, also observe how the game sites capture your attention and draw you back into playing other games. Ask a friend to do this with you so you can compare observations.

Write down your answers to these basic questions:

Which game did you choose?

_____

How long did you play?

_____

Would you play it again?

_____

How did the game site draw you in when you were choosing a game?

_____

_____

What was the first reachable goal, and how did it impact your motivation to play?

_____

_____

How did the feedback from your actions keep you engaged?

_____

_____

Were you aware of your progress in the game? Did it keep you playing?

_____

_____

What did you notice about the increased challenges in the game?

_____

_____

How did uncertainty within the game play keep you engaged?

_____

_____

What have you learned about how gaming publishers keep you engaged?

_____

_____

more to do

Fighting the lure of video games and technology is not easy. Even if you want to have more time for nontech activities, you'll have to work hard to do so. The following list of ideas has been developed by people who have struggled to put away their games and screens. Try one or two of these ideas at a time and come back to this activity in a few weeks to try some others.

As you try each suggestion, rate how helpful it is for you, using a scale from 1 (not at all helpful to 10 (very helpful). On the blank lines, write a sentence or two about why you rated the activity as you did.

Make mealtime a video-game–free time. Do not rush through meals to get back to gaming. Give yourself at least thirty minutes for meals.

1   2   3   4   5   6   7   8   9   10

_____

_____

Prior to playing a multiplayer game with friends, set a time you want to be done. This time limit can reduce peer pressure to continue playing and is important to ensure that you get enough sleep.

1   2   3   4   5   6   7   8   9   10

_____

_____

Find ways to transition easily away from your game play; for example, by playing prior to a set mealtime, having another fun activity that always follows game play, or scheduling a lesson or event following game play.

1   2   3   4   5   6   7   8   9   10

_____

_____

Make yourself get outside on a daily basis. Nature-based activities have positive effects on concentration, learning, and mood.

1   2   3   4   5   6   7   8   9   10

_____

_____

Work very hard to develop new hobbies. Consider your video-game play as one of many hobbies.

1   2   3   4   5   6   7   8   9   10

_____

_____

Give yourself realistic time limits for your game play that allow you time for fun and time for other activities. One way is to set an overall time limit for the day and to divide it into two or three periods. For example, you could give yourself ninety minutes overall, with sixty- and thirty-minute sessions.

1   2   3   4   5   6   7   8   9   10

_____

_____

25 strategies for distraction

Madison has always been a tech geek. She was twelve when she finally convinced her parents to get her an iPhone. Once she got it, she wouldn't go anywhere without it. She used it for playing games with her friends and could spend hours on social media, sharing pictures on Instagram, and texting nonstop. When she got a bit older, she discovered music online and downloaded Spotify. She became an expert among her friends on the best new music and games. All this engagement sometimes created too much drama, and because she didn't want to miss out on anything, homework could take longer due to interruptions.

One day, Madison lost her phone. While she had misplaced it a few times in the past, this time it was truly lost, and her parents were not interested in getting her a new phone right away. They were very concerned about her difficulty completing her homework and blamed her cell phone use for distracting her. Their reaction forced her to consider how much time she was spending on the phone playing games and engaging on social media. She decided that when she got a new phone, she would use it differently. She vowed to be more thoughtful about her game and social media use and to cut down on her screen time.

for you to know

If you wonder whether screen time is always good for you, you're not alone. In a 2018 study, the Pew Research Center reported that about 70 percent of teenagers interviewed about their screen use recognized that not all screen time is good for them. They described it as causing the spread of rumors, harming relationships, presenting distractions, increasing peer pressure, and even sometimes resulting in mental health issues. Many teenagers also described concerns about screen-time distractions related to their performance at school. Some even worried about the potential of being addicted to their phones.

This is not to say that they don't see the positive aspects of screen time, such as having fun playing video games, connecting with friends and family, finding out news and information about the world, and meeting people with similar interests. Adults may think that teens want to spend all their time on their phones, but that isn't the case. More than half of teens interviewed want to cut down on their screen time. They want to have more control over their phones and be less distracted by the games, social media, and stimulation from their technology.

Do you sleep with your phone? About 40 percent of teens do. Phones are hard to put away. Your cell phone can keep you entertained nonstop with games, social media, and videos. They are ever present and difficult to ignore. As you read in activity 24, part of the reason for this is how technology companies have designed hardware and software. But the other reason you can't ignore your cell phone and your other technology has to do with how you use it. And as you know, it can be a distraction and get in the way of doing other important things in your life.

for you to do

The following set of strategies was generated by the teenagers who were interviewed for this book. Read through all of them and rank them from 1 to 6, with 1 being the approach you think would be most helpful to *you*. Then give it a try and describe your experiences on the lines below. Try at least three of these ideas. Even if they don't work perfectly, they might be helpful in reducing the distraction of your screens.

_____ Put your phone on Do Not Disturb while you're doing your homework so you cannot hear notifications.

_____ Reward yourself with video-game play after you've accomplished other things (homework, chores, exercise) you need to do.

_____ Give yourself designated times to check social media or to game with your friends. Slowly decrease the amount of time you do either at any one point in time.

_____ Put on music on your phone and turn off notifications.

_____ Delete social media from your phone and use it only on other devices.

_____ Choose not to play video games or use other technologies during specific times when these are most disruptive for you; for example, at night because technologies interfere with your sleep, or when you typically do homework.

How well did your first choice work, and how might you improve upon it?

_____

_____

How well did your second choice work, and how might you improve upon it?

_____

_____

How well did your third choice work, and how might you improve upon it?

_____

_____

more to do

Enlist your parents, friends, or technology to reduce the distractions of gaming and technology rather than trying to do this on your own. As above, rank these strategies from 1 to 6, with 1 being the approach you think would be most helpful to *you*. Then give it a try and describe your experiences on the lines below. Try out at least three of these ideas. Even if they don't work perfectly, they might be helpful in reducing the distraction of your screens.

_____ Ask your parents to keep your cell phone for a set amount of time (perhaps thirty to sixty minutes) while you're studying.

_____ Use a phone holder that covers your screen and headphone jack, so they are less accessible.

_____ Study with a friend and agree to hold each other accountable for sustaining your focus and not allowing yourselves to get engaged with gaming or social media.

_____ Leave your cell phone in your car or room so you don't have it with you when you go to other places.

_____ Use a browser extension or app that restricts your access to specific games, sites, and social media. These are often called digital distraction tools.

_____ Use an old-fashioned timer or an alarm on your phone to set a specified amount of time when all other devices and games are shut down. (Our teen advisers suggest a minimum of thirty minutes, and preferably forty-five to sixty minutes.)

How well did your first choice work, and how might you improve upon it?

_____

_____

How well did your second choice work, and how might you improve upon it?

_____

_____

How well did your third choice work, and how might you improve upon it?

_____

_____

balancing your digital play with a healthy play diet 26

Ruben was always working at getting better at everything. He was very competitive and wanted to beat his friends at sports, board games such as Scrabble, and even in classic pinball machine games. As he got older and taller, he realized that he could become a good basketball player. But when he was in tenth grade, he began to spend most of his time indoors playing massive multiplayer online role-playing games (MMORPGs). He tried a lot of these games, including Star Wars: The Old Republic *and* World of Warcraft, *and became hooked on* Guild Wars 2. *Role-playing games suited Ruben's inclination to work hard. The more time and effort he put into the game, the more progress he could make. By the time he got to the eleventh grade, he was spending most of his after-school time playing* Guild Wars 2. *Between game play, social media with friends, and squeezing in homework, Ruben barely had time to sleep, and he decided to quit the basketball team.*

Ruben's mother expressed concerns that he was too focused on video-game play, and his friends told him the same thing. When Ruben found himself feeling depressed, he knew it was time for a change. The first thing he did was to get out of his room and spend more time outdoors and playing sports with his friends. This had immediate positive effects, and he began making more changes from that point on.

for you to know

The most powerful way children learn is through their play. Opportunities for play are not as common as you move into your teens, but play remains important as a chance for learning. Playing video games, using apps and social media, and engaging in other screen-based activities are all considered to be forms of play. In this book, we refer to this as "digital play." While some experts do not place much value on digital play, the perspective we take in this book is that it is one of the more potent forms of play for learning in the twenty-first century.

Digital play can be crucial for learning problem-solving, academic, social, and emotional skills. But if it is your only form of play, you'll miss out on many other opportunities for learning and won't have as much fun and as many connections with others.

One of the best ways to avoid being overloaded by video games is to engage in different kinds of play. In this book, play is divided into five categories that are important for learning and happiness: *social play* (spending time with other people), *physical play* (sports, exercise, being outdoors), *creative play* (artistic, imaginative, and pretend activities), *unstructured play* (a form of free play without any particular rules), and *digital play* (which involves the use of video games, social media, and other screen-based technologies).

Achieving a healthy play diet, in which digital play is an important part of your play activities but not the only one, is key. Play diets vary based upon your interests, opportunities, and personal strengths. Having some balance in your play diet is healthier for your physical, mental, emotional, and cognitive well-being.

for you to do

Over the course of one week, complete this chart to see how you spend your play time. At the end of each day, record the approximate number of minutes you engaged in each of type of the different forms of play, and write the total in the column on the right. (You can use the definitions you just read to help you.) At the end of the week, add up how much time you spent in each type of play, and write the total in the bottom row. You can do this in the following chart (or download a copy at http://www.newharbinger.com/45519) or use your cell phone to collect this information via a time tracker app. It can be difficult to keep an accurate gauge of your different forms of play because of the back-and-forth nature of your daily activities, so give your best estimate. In addition, some activities (for example, playing soccer with your friends) should count as physical *and* social play.

The purpose of this exercise is to inform you as to how you spend your playtime. Don't judge yourself but use this as an opportunity to step back and recognize where you put your energies.

How I Spend My Playtime

	Physical play	Social play	Free play	Creative play	Digital play	Total
Monday						
Tuesday						
Wednesday						
Thursday						
Friday						
Saturday						
Sunday						
Total						

more to do

Create your ideal play diet, where you consider your overall fun and health. You can use this chart or download a copy at http://www.newharbinger.com/45519. Imagine that you have eight hours of play time each day in which you could do anything you want. You do not have homework, a job, or any other responsibilities. You could play video games for eight hours or go to the beach with your friends for the day.

As you put in the hours for your play diet, be specific about what activity you would do in that play. For example, if you chose to play video games for four hours, you would write down a few of the games you might like to play. While you might want to spend all your time in front of a screen, we encourage you to consider the importance of a healthy and balanced play diet that fits your own interests.

My Ideal Play Diet

Type of play	Activity I'd choose	How long I'd do it
Physical play (exercise, sports, movement)		
Social play (peers, talking, family time, socializing)		
Free play (no rules or expectations, relaxing)		
Creative play (art, reading, cooking, drawing)		
Digital play (video games, tech, social media, internet)		

Play diets are individual lifestyle choices. Some of you love to hang out with friends, while others may cherish their alone time. An ideal play diet has some balance, so that over the course of a week, you have an opportunity for many types of play. Try to combine types of play. For example, cooking a meal with your friends involves both social and creative play. While your ideal play diet should be unique to you, our suggestions, based on research on health, happiness, and psychological adjustment, indicate the need for physical and social play on a daily basis.

27 creativity in a play diet

Hanna is a sixteen-year-old aspiring artist and designer. As a young child, she loved playing with her Barbie dolls, and when she got older, she decided she could design and make better clothing for her dolls than she could buy at the store. In elementary school, she played hair- and clothing-design video games and loved any game that involved cake and pastry decoration. Although in real life she helped her mother with preparation for dinner parties, most of her creative energies were in her game play. Her mind was often in the clouds, designing new clothing and food presentations.

When she got into her teens, she discovered computer-assisted design (CAD). She could sit in front of the computer for hours using her creative skills and often became totally absorbed in increasingly complex designs. She was fascinated by using 3-D printing to display her designs, which inspired her to want to take her designs and make them real. She decided to focus on designing cakes and pastries with her CAD programs and soon became well-known, and handsomely paid, for her spectacular designs.

for you to know

Experts describe two crucial skill sets for work in the decades to come: technology expertise and problem-solving/creativity/critical-thinking skills. You use both of these skill sets when you're playing video games, searching the internet, or navigating software and social media. It's fairly easy to recognize the places you use tech skills and how you apply them to using different games and apps, but you might be less aware of the problem-solving skills required in games and the use of other technologies.

Consider the problem-solving skills you use when searching the internet for a school project. You need to plan for the initial search terms you'll use, then be flexible and make changes to find the best information. You need to be organized so your information is all in one place. You may also need to be creative to find images, videos, or other methods to complete your report. You need to use judgment skills to determine what is most important for your project.

for you to do

Spend about sixty minutes playing a sandbox game such as *Minecraft, Assassin's Creed,* or *Grand Theft Auto,* and create a scenario with buildings, people, and dangers. Observe how you start with nothing, obtain tools and materials, and then engage in a set of actions.

For about sixty minutes, do the same thing without technological tools: draw a picture, find materials to build something, or write a story that matches your sandbox scenario. Don't judge your creations; allow yourself to make mistakes and changes. Then respond to these questions:

What game did you choose? _____

What type of nontech activity did you choose? _____

What did you do in your video-game play that involved creativity?

_____

_____

What did you do in your nontech play that involved creativity?

_____

_____

Which was more fun, and why?

_____

_____

Where did you need to be more creative, and why?

_____

_____

How did the level of detail compare?

_____

_____

Which required more of your brainpower, and why?

_____

_____

Which was easier to start and complete, and why?

_____

_____

List three ways in which nontech activities helped you be creative.

1. _____

2. _____

3. _____

List three ways in which the sandbox game helped you be creative.

1. _____

2. _____

3. _____

more to do

In this thought experiment, you'll toss away reality and use your creativity. Technology has always been one of the drivers of creativity. Consider how the printing press created the opportunity for more books to be published or how the invention of the semiconductor led to the computer, the cell phone, and many other technologies. Twenty-first century technologies are opening many new areas for creative thought and change. Futurists see virtual reality, blockchain, artificial intelligence, and robotics as among the most important new technologies.

Choose one of these emerging technologies or find another to explore for this activity. Spend an hour learning more about how the technology you choose is likely to play a role in your future.

Which technology did you choose to explore?

_____

What were the three most surprising things you learned in your research about this technology?

1. _____

2. _____

3. _____

Then use your imagination and creative mind to consider how that technology might impact your future in the following areas.

Work (How will the technology create new jobs, change existing jobs, or require a new set of skills?)

1. _____

2. _____

3. _____

Entertainment and leisure (How will the technology create new forms of fun and play? Will it be widely available, and how will it impact your choice of activities?)

1. _____

2. _____

3. _____

Connection with nature (How will the technology help you be involved with the natural world, explore the outdoors, and impact the environment?)

1. _____

2. _____

3. _____

Relationships with others (How will the technology connect people directly or result in different types of relationships?)

1. _____

2. _____

3. _____

nature and unstructured playtime 28

Neil was always interested in anything related to biology. As a preschooler, he loved playing with animals and exploring the woods for worms, snakes, and frogs. When it came time to dissect a frog in biology class, he was the first to volunteer. Everyone assumed he'd eventually become a doctor because of his interest in bodies and how they worked.

In high school, Neil was drawn to biology and other sciences. While he loved nature, he had never planted a garden or shown any interest in how fruits and vegetables grow. He didn't even like to spend time relaxing outdoors. But that was before he became hooked on playing Farmville. *His parents thought he might forgo a career in medicine and want to become a farmer instead. He began studying the impact of organic farming, became outspoken about the use of pesticides, and convinced his parents to plow over half their backyard to create an organic garden so they could eat healthier foods.*

for you to know

Video games in modest amounts can be good for you. Being out in nature, even in *large* amounts, is good for you as well. That's not just the advice of your parents when they tell you to go outside and get some fresh air. Many studies show that people who spend time outdoors are less likely to be depressed. It's as easy as just playing outside. Elementary school kids who go out for recess and play in a natural setting pay better attention and learn more. Being outdoors boosts your energy and immune system.

The movement to get back to nature has some of its basis in eating more natural and organic foods. Interests in farming, gardening, and taking care of the environment are important concerns for future generations, including yours. There are concerns that your generation might become overly involved with virtual reality or other newer technologies that make the indoors feel like the outdoors. All the evidence supports spending as much unstructured time in nature as possible.

for you to do

An appreciation of nature and being outdoors does not mean you cannot like video games and other technologies. One of the aims of this book is to help you use your interest in games and technology to develop other passions, such as being out in nature. Many video games take place in a naturalistic setting that helps gamers explore different types of terrain, animals, and landscapes. There are also increasing numbers of smaller indie video games that focus on environmental issues designed to promote a greater love and understanding of nature.

In this activity, you'll play a video game that engages you in the appreciation of nature or helps you understand the challenges facing our environment. Get one of the virtual reality simulators from PlayStation VR for an intense nature experience or download a nature-based game through the Games for Change organization. If you don't have access to a PlayStation VR or other headset, use a simple VR application that employs your phone for a VR experience.

After you play the game, respond to these questions:

What game did you play?

_____

How does playing the game or simulator make you want to explore nature?

_____

_____

What do you want to learn more about as a result of your game play?

_____

_____

How could you combine your interest in video gaming and technology with getting out in nature?

_____

_____

more to do

For this activity, take a long hike in a local park or along a trail, paying particular attention to nature as you see it.

For the first part of your hike, turn off all devices and don't pay attention to anything electronic. Try to stay fully focused on what you're doing. Be in the moment. Consider this unstructured play.

During the second part of your hike, turn on your cell phone and allow yourself to respond to calls, texts, and alerts and to play social games or use it for taking pictures of what you're doing.

At the end of the hike, take a few minutes to compare and contrast the two parts of your hike.

What differences did you notice between the nontech access as opposed to the tech access parts of your hike?

_____

_____

To what degree did the absence of technology help you appreciate what you were experiencing?

_____

_____

To what degree did having your camera available help you appreciate what you were doing?

_____

_____

How did access to your technology affect how you'll describe and report your experiences to others?

_____

_____

How did having access to your cell phone and gaming enhance your hike?

_____

_____

can game play inspire physical play?

Seth came from a family of athletes. His mother was a long-distance runner, and his brothers were both excellent soccer players. His father was the best athlete of all and had never lost a game of one-on-one basketball to any of his sons. Seth's favorite sport was also basketball. When he was younger, all he wanted to do was shoot baskets.

In middle school, his parents drove him and his siblings to sports practice almost every day. And when he wasn't going to sports practice, he was playing sports video games such as FIFA soccer and NBA 2K games. He found that playing sports video games encouraged him to be out on the field more often. However, as he got older, he began spending more time playing video games and less time playing sports. In high school, he no longer wanted to be on the soccer team and needed to be encouraged to try out for the basketball team. He was embarrassed to tell his parents that he didn't want to be on the team because he had more fun playing video games with his friends than going to practice. In tenth grade, he didn't make the cut on the basketball team, mostly because he didn't practice regularly. Eventually, after months of playing video games and not exercising, he noticed he was getting out of shape and decided to find a better balance between his video-game play and his interest in sports.

for you to know

Kids who play sports video games usually don't spend all their time staring at a screen. In fact, those who play sports video games are more likely than their friends to spend more time playing actual sports. There are many studies indicating that kids who play sports video games are motivated to get better at real-life sports. Sports video-game players learn about game strategies and often model themselves after the professional players who are the stars of the video games.

One of the main messages of this book is the importance of teenagers and their parents balancing video-game play with other activities. Perhaps the most significant of these other activities is physical fitness and exercise. It's pretty simple. Regular vigorous exercise improves physical and mental health and, as a bonus, improves attention, memory, problem solving, and learning. Playing sports video games often encourages kids to exercise and improve their ability to study more effectively, remember what they've learned, and be more efficient in completing their schoolwork. They're also better able to handle stress.

for you to do

Make a commitment to regular exercise by choosing a sport or type of exercise you enjoy. Over the next two weeks, try to do it every day or, at a minimum, four times a week. It doesn't matter if it is an indoor or outside activity; just choose something you can do without too much travel or expense. Walk, run, bike, skateboard, go to the gym, do yoga, lift weights, play basketball, or swim—whatever engages you!

Do this for a minimum of forty-five minutes each time. If you're just beginning regular exercise, start a bit slower, and try to work up to forty-five minutes a session by the end of the first week. Keep track of your exercise in the following chart; you can download copies at http://www.newharbinger.com/45519. (One hint: Ask a friend or family member to do this with you. You may find that the social aspect is a powerful motivator to keep you exercising.)

My Exercise Record

Week number: _____   Type of exercise: _____

	Amount of time
Day 1	
Day 2	
Day 3	
Day 4	
Day 5	
Day 6	
Day 7	

At the end of each week, respond to these questions.

How do you feel physically? _____

Have you observed any change in your sleeping?

_____

Do you have more or less energy, and when do you notice any changes?

_____

Have you lost any weight or gained any muscle mass?

_____

more to do

Once you get into the routine of exercise, it will be important to monitor your exercise and other activities. Self-observation is one of the best tools for self-improvement. Use a fitness monitor or app (these are inexpensive and often available as an app on your phone) to keep track of your exercise. Monitor steps if appropriate; the common recommendation is to take about ten thousand steps a day. Otherwise, keep track of how much weight you lift, how much time you play a sport, or how many laps you swim to show you how you're progressing and help you connect your physical, emotional, and focusing skills to exercise.

Instead of commenting on physical changes due to exercise, explore the following areas:

What activities are you spending less time on than before because you're exercising?

_____

_____

_____

What do you notice about your attention and clarity of thought in the hour after you exercise?

_____

_____

_____

How has exercise impacted your study habits?

_____

_____

_____

What changes, if any, have you observed in your ability to remember, manage your time, or control your emotions?

_____

_____

_____

30 games as social play

Russ was what's called an old soul, fifteen going on fifty. Not only was he wise beyond his years, but, according to his friends, he also sometimes acted like an old man. His favorite thing to do with his friends was to play history-based video games, particularly those set in the Middle Ages. The friends called themselves the "Friars" when games required a team. Russ and his friends got together almost every afternoon and played video games for three or four hours a night. The games helped them stay more connected, and game play was often their topic of discussion in school the next day.

One day Russ's friend Les began questioning his buddies about whether they were spending too much time playing video games. Up until then, they had been having so much fun with each other that they never thought about it. But everyone always listened to Les, so they began to cut down on their game play on school days and found that their friendship became even better when they discovered a few new activities to do together.

for you to know

Having meaningful long-term relationships with other people is one of the best predictors of happiness and psychological adjustment for people of all ages. Regular contact with friends, engagement in activities with others, and talking with friends and family help counteract depression and lead to people feeling more productive, experiencing less physical illness, and living longer.

While scientists have not done much research about the impact of meaningful long-term online relationships, there is reason to think that similar benefits may be found in this area. Playing video games with friends is an everyday experience for many younger people and another way to help form and maintain relationships.

Gaming together also gives you an opportunity to talk about things beyond gaming. Whether you're using Discord or another video and text chat, online gaming opens a door to discussion with your peers. More than half of teenagers report that they count on their friends for guidance and decision making and are willing to share information about things they don't want to talk about with their parents—issues such as sexuality, alcohol use, or even how much they play video games.

for you to do

Start a conversation with friends you regularly play online team video games with, talking about how you view gaming in your life. Having a written record of this conversation could be fascinating (and fun!) to look back on in later years. If you'd like to keep a written record, you can download a copy of the questions at http://www. newharbinger.com/45519 and have everyone in the group write down their responses.

Make it an open-ended discussion, but start by asking what they think the future impact of playing these games will be on their lives. Here are some additional questions you might ask:

What do you think has been the best thing to happen to us as a group due to playing video games together?

_____

_____

_____

How has playing video games together impacted our friendship?

_____

_____

_____

What have we learned from each other by playing video games together?

_____

_____

_____

How might our history of playing games together as teenagers impact our future friendship?

_____

_____

_____

What are the drawbacks of spending some of our time playing video games together?

_____

_____

_____

more to do

Think about a friend from the past you would like to reconnect with. Through social media or someone you both know, reach out to that friend.

Invite your old friend to play a social game such as Words with Friends. There are also many other social games on iPhones or Android phones that are fun and super easy to use. If the person does not respond, try again or reach out to someone else. This activity is designed to see what the experience is like for you.

As an alternative, arrange to do this with your grandparents. Tell them you can help them find and connect with old friends online. They might want to start with a phone call or a snail-mail letter to make the initial connection. If this is successful, suggest they set up an online game with the friends and help them make this happen. They might find that they share an interest such as playing bridge, chess, or a different card game online. If this works, ask questions and observe. See how your grandparents choose to sustain future communication, how they share information about themselves and their family, and how they use technology to reestablish old friendships.

What was it like for you to reconnect?

_____

_____

What was the reaction of the people you reconnected with?

_____

_____

What did you talk about?

_____

_____

How does reaching out with a social video game compare to seeing someone from your past in real life?

_____

_____

References

Alter, A. 2017. *Irresistible: The Rise of Addictive Technology and the Business of Keeping Us Hooked*. New York: Penguin Press.

Anderson, M., and J. Jiang. 2018. "Teens, Social Media & Technology." *Pew Research Center*. https://www.pewresearch.org/internet/2018/05/31/teens-social-media-technology-2018/.

"Blue Light Has a Dark Side." 2018. *Harvard Health Letter*. https://www.health.harvard.edu/staying-healthy/blue-light-has-a-dark-side.

Gentile, D. A., K. Bailey, D. Bavelier, J. F. Brockmyer, H. Cash, S. M. Coyne, et al. 2017. "Internet Gaming Disorder in Children and Adolescents." *Pediatrics*, 140(Supplement 2): S81–S85.

Granic, I., A. Lobel, and R. C. Engels. 2014. "The Benefits of Playing Video Games." *American Psychologist* 69(1): 66.

Jiang, J. 2018. "How Teens and Parents Navigate Screen Time and Device Distractions. *Pew Research Center*. https://www.pewresearch.org/internet/2018/08/22/how-teens-and-parents-navigate-screen-time-and-device-distractions/.

Lauricella, A. R., D. P. Cingel, L. Beaudoin-Ryan, M. B. Robb, M. Saphir, and E. A. Wartella. 2016. *The Common Sense Census: Plugged-in Parents of Tweens and Teens*. Common Sense Media.

McGonigal, J. 2011. *Reality Is Broken: Why Games Make Us Better and How They Can Change the World*. New York: Penguin Press.

"Multitasking: Switching Costs." 2019. *American Psychological Association*. https://www. apa.org/research/action/multitask.

Rideout, V. J. 2015. *The Common Sense Census: Media Use by Tweens and Teens*. Common Sense Media.

Robb, M. R. 2019. *The New Normal: Parents, Teens, Screens, and Sleep in the United States*. Common Sense Media.

Russ, S. W., and J. A. Dillon. 2011. "Changes in Children's Pretend Play Over Two Decades." *Creativity Research Journal* 23(4): 330–338.

Randy Kulman, PhD, is a clinical child psychologist who has worked with kids and families for the past thirty years, and has become a leading expert on the use of digital technologies for improving thinking skills in children. He is founder and president of the technology website, LearningWorks for Kids, an online platform for informing and instructing parents on how to enrich and enhance their kids' digital playtime. His blog, *Screen Play,* on www.psychologytoday.com helps kids and parents balance their screen time with other activities. He is author of *Train Your Brain for Success* and *Playing Smarter in a Digital World*. Learn more at learningworksforkids.com.

More ⏱ Instant Help Books for Teens

An Imprint of New Harbinger Publications

**THE EXECUTIVE FUNCTIONING
WORKBOOK FOR TEENS**

Help for Unprepared, Late &
Scattered Teens

978-1608826568 / US $17.95

**THE STRESS REDUCTION
WORKBOOK FOR TEENS,
SECOND EDITION**

Mindfulness Skills to Help You
Deal with Stress

978-1684030187 / US $16.95

THE GRIT GUIDE FOR TEENS

A Workbook to Help You Build
Perseverance, Self-Control &
a Growth Mindset

978-1626258563 / US $16.95

**THE ANGER WORKBOOK FOR
TEENS, SECOND EDITION**

Activities to Help You Deal with
Anger & Frustration

978-1684032457 / US $17.95

**DON'T LET YOUR EMOTIONS
RUN YOUR LIFE FOR TEENS**

Dialectical Behavior Therapy Skills
for Helping You Manage Mood
Swings, Control Angry Outbursts &
Get Along with Others

978-1684037360 / US $18.95

**THE SOCIAL MEDIA
WORKBOOK FOR TEENS**

Skills to Help You Balance
Screen Time, Manage Stress &
Take Charge of Your Life

978-1684031900 / US $16.95

newharbingerpublications

1-800-748-6273 / newharbinger.com

(VISA, MC, AMEX / prices subject to change without notice)

Follow Us 📷 👍 🐦 ▶️ 📌 in

Don't miss out on new books in the subjects that interest you.
Sign up for our **Book Alerts** at **newharbinger.com/bookalerts** 🖱️

Register your **new harbinger** titles for additional benefits!

When you register your **new harbinger** title—purchased in any format, from any source—you get access to benefits like the following:

- Downloadable accessories like printable worksheets and extra content

- Instructional videos and audio files

- Information about updates, corrections, and new editions

Not every title has accessories, but we're adding new material all the time.

Access free accessories in 3 easy steps:

1. Sign in at NewHarbinger.com (or **register** to create an account).

2. Click on **register a book**. Search for your title and click the **register** button when it appears.

3. Click on the **book cover or title** to go to its details page. Click on **accessories** to view and access files.

That's all there is to it!

If you need help, visit:

NewHarbinger.com/accessories

new harbinger
CELEBRATING
40 YEARS